D0064528

SOME SUNNY DAY

Dear Grandma,

Hope you enjoy this book + your 94th birthday

Lot of Love + Hugs

Lorna, Kevin, Stephanie, Jorene + Joel.

Dame Vera Lynn

SOME SUNNY DAY

MY AUTOBIOGRAPHY

HARPER

HARPER

an imprint of
HarperCollins*Publishers*
77–85 Fulham Palace Road
Hammersmith, London W6 8JB

www.harpercollins.co.uk

First published by HarperCollins*Publishers* 2009
This edition 2010

1

Sections of this book were previously published
under the title *Vocal Refrain* in 1975.

The author asserts the moral right to
be identified as the author of this work

A catalogue record of this book is
available from the British Library

ISBN 978-0-00-731891-9

Printed and bound in Great Britain by
Clays Ltd, St Ives plc

Mixed Sources
Product group from well-managed
forests and other controlled sources
www.fsc.org   Cert no. SW-COC-1806
© 1996 Forest Stewardship Council

FSC is a non-profit international organisation established to promote the
responsible management of the world's forests. Products carrying the FSC
label are independently certified to assure consumers that they come
from forests that are managed to meet the social, economic and
ecological needs of present and future generations.

Find out more about HarperCollins and the environment at
www.harpercollins.co.uk/green

PICTURE CREDITS

All photographs have been supplied by and are
copyright of the author and her family, with the exception of:
Getty Images, pp. 6b, 11b, 13t, 13b, 15t; Topfoto, pp. 7t, 14b, 15b.

While every effort has been made to trace the owners of copyright
material reproduced herein, the publishers would like to apologise
for any omissions and will be pleased to incorporate missing
acknowledgements in any future correspondence.

Contents

To my wonderful Harry, with whom I was so fortunate
to share my life for all those years.

And to 'The Boys', to whom we all owe so much –
your spirit and humour live with me to this day.
Never forgotten.

Acknowledgements

I must thank all my family, of course, for their constant support and love.

And there are too many others whom I have met and worked with over the years to thank here, so I will mention just three: my dear friend Wally Ridley, for his help in those Denmark Street days; Joe Loss, for selecting me for my first broadcast; and Norman Newell, who produced all my early records. These three men were instrumental in making my life the extraordinary event that it has been.

Introduction

Iwill always remember the moment war was declared at the beginning of September 1939. I was sitting in the garden of the new house I had bought in Barking with Mum and Dad. Life was going well for me: I was singing with Bert Ambrose's band, fulfilling what was really the only ambition I had ever had: to be the best singer with the best band in the land. Before the announcement came, anyone would have told you that times were not easy, but my life was certainly not bad.

On that day I remember we were all drinking tea in the garden, my dad sitting in his deckchair as he loved to do. He was always brown from sitting in the sun. Naturally we had the radio on all the time because everyone was interested in what was going on. For weeks everyone had been on tenterhooks, not knowing what was going to come. And that's when I heard the news. The first thought that came into my head was a selfish one: Oh dear. There goes my singing career. Everything I have dreamed of, I thought to myself, is over. The men – including all the musicians I knew in the band – would all be going away to fight. And I would be headed straight for the

1

munitions factory. I was only twenty-two. It seemed like the end of my world.

At that point no one thought that entertainment would become essential during the war. And I certainly never thought I would have the chance to continue singing. I was already very familiar with the words to 'We'll Meet Again' by then, but I had no idea that that particular song would become the tune people most associated with the war era. Or that my voice would become the one that most reminded people of the hope for the future we needed to have at that time.

Seven decades later I remember that day as clearly as if it were yesterday. So it makes me especially proud and honoured to know that all these years later people still want to mark the anniversary. This year, 2009, marks seventy years since the outbreak of the war as well as the sixty-fifth anniversary of D-Day, the biggest wartime operation ever. It's difficult for me to believe that it was that many years ago, because in my mind there are times when it feels so recent. It thrills me to know that people still remember and still care. It's so important.

This year also marks exactly seventy years since I first sang that well-known song, the one that made my name, on tour with Ambrose's band in the autumn of 1939. Ironically, precisely a year before that, I was on stage while history was being made. On 29 September 1938 I was performing at the Hammersmith Palais in London. Meanwhile the British Prime Minister, Neville Chamberlain, was in Munich for a meeting with Hitler. This was the meeting where Chamberlain believed he had received the reassurance that there would be 'peace for our time'. Which, as we know now, unravelled within the space of the next twelve months.

In many ways I feel honoured and privileged to have become a symbol of that era. It's very humbling. But there have been times in my life when I have felt uncomfortable about it too: it is something to live up to when people call you a national treasure, and that is certainly not an expression I would use myself. I just see myself as someone who found herself in the right place at the right time – or perhaps we should call it the wrong time – and I just happened to have a voice which suited the era and, somehow or other, has stood the test of time.

I'm told that schoolchildren today still learn the words to 'We'll Meet Again'. That thrills me. It seems that the songs I am remembered for from the war have passed from generation to generation, so that young people today know about them. I still feel a part of things. I have kept myself busy in my semi-retirement: I have a garden I look after (with help) and I still drive – but only locally. I feel fortunate that I'm in a position where for the past thirty years I have been able to spend time on the charities I support, such as Breast Cancer Research and my trust, which helps children with cerebral palsy. And, of course, I still like to help organizations such as the Royal British Legion, which supports ex-servicemen.

Almost forty years ago I published an earlier version of my memoirs. This was at a time when I was still appearing regularly in my own television show and – astonishingly to me – my career was still going strong some thirty years after the war. Towards the end of that decade – the 1970s – I began the slow process towards retirement, although I have never really wanted to step completely out of the spotlight. Now that I am ninety-two, barely a week goes by without someone asking me to cut a ribbon at some event or other, and I am more than happy to oblige.

At my ripe old age, though, I felt it was time to revisit that era properly and get everything down on paper in a final account. I have also found that as the years pass I remember some things with a clarity that I didn't have before. My trip to Burma, for example, looms large in my memories as one of the pivotal moments of my life. I didn't really understand that when I was in my fifties. In this book, for the first time I have been able to recall that trip in a lot more detail – and I even found the red leather Collins diary I carried with me throughout. I'm particularly fond of that little diary, because I wasn't supposed to keep it: we were not allowed to take any notes in case they fell into enemy hands. I wrote in it in tiny spidery handwriting that I thought the enemy would never be able to read.

Perhaps unsurprisingly, a lot of the events I am involved with today revolve around wartime. I still attend many charity events and veterans' anniversaries, and often the ones that I find most moving are to do with Burma. Five years ago I attended a grand reunion for Burma veterans at London's Imperial War Museum. It was the sixtieth anniversary of a number of decisive battles fought by the 'Forgotten' Fourteenth Army in the vicious Burma jungle campaign. More than a hundred veterans attended, many in their eighties and nineties. To my astonishment, there was one man there I recognized, although I wouldn't have known his name – Neville Hogan. It turns out I met him on my tour of Burma in 1944. I sang a concert for the Second Battalion Burma Rifles. He was sick in hospital at the time and I visited him there. When I asked him what I could do for him, he said, 'A kiss.' I held his hand and kissed him on the forehead.

At the reunion he was now eighty and I was eighty-seven. I kissed him again on the forehead. He remembered my visit to his camp vividly and told a reporter about it afterwards: 'Dame Vera came into the room and visited every soldier individually. She stood at the side of the bed and asked each one if she could have anything sent over for them. She was fantastic. She used to come and play off the side of a truck and boost everyone's morale.' I'm very proud of that. To think that I entertained audiences from 2,000 to 6,000 in that blazing heat. The boys would just come out of the jungle and sit there for hours waiting until we arrived and then slip back in once we'd left. What I enjoyed most, though – and still do now – was chatting to the troops. What they needed was a contact from home rather than a concert. I knew it was my place to provide that. It was the least I could do. When I talked to the men and women who served at war about their thoughts and how they felt about going into action, many of them would just shrug, saying, 'It's what we are trained to do.' Their humility was matched only by their courage, honour and duty.

That was their vocation; singing was mine. People have always been amazed to learn that I can't read music. I told a newspaper in 1943, 'I learn a tune pretty easily although I can't read music. I get the words into my head and then run them over and over again until I don't have to bother any more because they just come out naturally. Then I can think about the singing.' They called me 'a natural born singer, who sings like a thrush, sweetly and spontaneously'. And they added: 'There are plenty of people who can read music who could not sing like Vera in a thousand years. And there are not many who would not give their ability to read music for a voice like hers.'

It makes me laugh to read what else I told them for that article: that I wanted to retire before long (seventy years later and I haven't really retired at all), that I wanted to get the garden going properly (that took another fifty years) and that I wanted 'a couple of kids, maybe, when I get time' (I had one daughter, Virginia, born in 1946; work got in the way of having the bigger family I had once dreamed of). My music publisher, Walter Ridley, added his thoughts at the time: 'The secret of the kid's success is that she's genuinely sincere and sounds it.'

I like to think that he was right and that is why my voice and my songs are remembered now. If, in any small way, that can go towards encouraging people to commemorate the sacrifice of those who fought in the Second World War, then I am glad. We should always carry on remembering what happened seventy years ago. Even now I am constantly inspired by the work and bravery of our servicemen and women. Simon Weston, for example, the hero who was badly burned during the sinking of the *Sir Galahad* during the Falklands conflict, has become a good friend of the family. Earlier this year (June 2009) I was with him at the opening of a new burns research laboratory at the Blond McIndoe Research Foundation. It is based at the Queen Victoria Hospital in East Grinstead, where Sir Archibald McIndoe treated hundreds of burned air crew during the Second World War. There were a lot of burns victims during the Second World War – I remember visiting so many of them myself – and centres like this continue to be invaluable even today. Many of them – like this one – are funded solely on charitable donations. I feel it's important for me to keep going if I can help in any way at all.

As I look back on my life, I am grateful to have survived that time and to be a symbol of an era which must never be forgotten. If that is my legacy, then I am proud of it. We still have servicemen and women serving abroad now and who knows when they will be called upon to fight for their country in the future? It's for the ones who are fighting now that we must always make sure that the ones who fought in the past are not forgotten.

As for me, although my last official public performance was in 1995 at the VE Day Golden Jubilee concert outside Buckingham Palace, people still seem to hold me in mind. I feel privileged to have done three Royal Variety shows across three decades – in 1960, 1975 and 1986 – and to have performed with some of the favourites of the last century: Bing Crosby, Morecambe and Wise, Cliff Richard. All in all it has been quite a journey for a plumber's daughter from East Ham who almost didn't make it to her third birthday.

CHAPTER ONE

Overture & Beginnings

The funny thing is, I don't remember singing as a tiny child. It's only from my press cuttings that I know that apparently I could sing five songs right through by the time I was two. And I'm sure that when I was two and a half my uncle George taught me two old favourites – 'K-K-K-Katy' and 'I'm Sorry I Made You Cry' – because I've been told this many times. But I believe that a person's life only really begins with what they can remember for themselves. So my story has got to start, strangely enough, with the time I nearly died. I was not quite three years old.

I have a recollection of being all on my own in some kind of a tent, surrounded by steaming kettles. I can't shake off the impression that the tent was out of doors. Wherever it was, it was certainly in East Ham Hospital, and I was in isolation there with a dangerous illness called diphtheric croup. The steam was part of the treatment, I suppose.

I found out when I was older that at one stage they didn't think I was going to live, and it's peculiar to look back now and realize that there very nearly wasn't anything to tell. I don't know how long they kept me in the tent, but I was in hospital for three months altogether, and came out in time for my third birthday in 1920.

By that time I'd missed Christmas, so I had my Christmas and birthday all in one, in March. Mum even got me a Christmas tree from somewhere. I was Vera Welch then, and we lived in Thackeray Road, East Ham. All my life most people have thought, Oh, Vera Lynn, she grew up in the East End. But it's not really the East End at all. East Ham is in fact classified as Essex. That ground-floor flat in Thackeray Road is my other earliest memory. I can see the little kitchen and wash-house now – especially the wash-house, where I went through a right terrible scrubbing from an aunt who'd come in to look after me. My mother had had to go off somewhere for the day – to make a visit to a hospital, I think – and this aunt was taking care of me, and when the time came for her to wash me she scrubbed and rubbed me dry so hard that I can feel the rough towelling even now, all these years later. In the kitchen was a high dresser along one wall, and that sticks in my memory because my brother knocked an egg-cup off it and broke it and got a clip round the ear for it.

These trivial incidents must have made a tremendous impression on me, for they remain vivid in my mind's eye after ninety years. I know for certain that they took place before I was four, because when I was four we moved to another of those straight, flat East Ham streets, Ladysmith Avenue, to share a house with my grandma. And there we would stay until 1938, when at the age of twenty-one I'd made enough progress as a singer to be able to buy a house for my mum and dad and myself not far away in Barking.

In many ways we were just another typical working-class family. We were a small family: just me, my brother Roger, who was three years older than me, my parents, and my grandma, of course. I have very few recollections of my parents' parents, although I have some beautiful old-fashioned pictures of them all. I vaguely remember my mother's father, who died when I was four years old. From the photographs you'd think that we were well off, because everyone was always dressed in their Sunday best if they were having their photograph taken or if they were going out somewhere special. There's a favourite shot I have of one of my aunts wearing a tweed suit, a fur tippet and a hat on the beach. I even have a photograph of my father on holiday in the countryside wearing what looks like a bowler hat. It was not because people were wealthy that they dressed like that: they just wore their best clothes to go out.

My mother, Annie, was a dressmaker and my father, Bertram, did all sorts of jobs. To this day I haven't the faintest idea how my parents met – I never asked them. They were just ordinary people to me. My mother was a bit smart, though, because of her dressmaking. She made all her own clothes. Before she was married, she worked for a London dressmaker who took on royal commissions. She was the one who taught me how to sew and make things properly. My father worked as a plumber and he'd been on the docks. In those days, you took any job you could get. That's how it was when I was a child. Despite this, my father was an easy-going man who liked to laugh – and he was a very good dancer.

That's what was unusual about my childhood in a way. Thinking back on it all now, I realize that the things which helped to determine that I would go on to have a career as a singer were part of my life very early on, even though they may not have stayed in my mind in the same way as the kettles and the wash-house and the rough towel and the broken egg-cup. We had quite a social life. There was Uncle George, my Dad's brother, who had taught me those songs and would even wake me up to sing them for him. He used to appear in the working men's clubs doing a George Robey impression, with a little round hat and the arched eyebrows; he had an act with his sister as well, and they wrote some of their own songs. Dad himself was very active in the East Ham Working Men's Club, and was master of ceremonies at the dances there on a Saturday night: I used to see him in his white gloves and patent pumps, calling out the names of the dances, and feel so proud of him. During the long period of the club-going days – almost the first two decades of my life – he worked not only in the docks, but also as a plumber's mate, as a glass blower, at the Co-op and, during the Depression, sometimes not at all; but whatever he was doing, I think it was his club activities he really lived for – his darts, his billiards and above all his dancing. In fact the whole family was very socially minded, and I was taken to the club as a matter of course from my very earliest childhood. Now I come to think of it, it was at a concert in the East Ham club that I was first taken ill that time.

Even after we moved to Ladysmith Avenue and lived with my grandma, Margaret Martin, my mother's mother, there was never any question of leaving me at home. For a start,

Grandma always came with us anyway, until she got too old, but that had nothing to do with it – it was simply the accepted thing that we should all go as a family. So, what with my dad being master of ceremonies at the dances, and one of his sisters being on the music-hall stage in a small way, and Uncle George singing his songs and doing his George Robey act, and Mum occasionally seeing to some of the club bar work and the catering ('There's money in cups of tea,' she used to say in her practical way), I got accustomed very early to the idea of helping to provide entertainment.

Besides, we were a great family for singing: there were good voices on both sides, and no reluctance to use them. Grandma had a lovely voice, untrained, but much more of a concert performer's voice than the voices of the rest of us. She used to sing ballads like the popular 'Thora', by Stephen Adams, and 'Until', and she still sang at the party we gave for her eighty-fourth birthday. Dad had a good voice and his party piece was 'Laugh and the world will be smiling, weep and you're weeping alone'. There always seemed to be sing-song parties going on round at my other grandmother's in Gillett Avenue – which was the next road – with my aunt at the piano and everybody doing something.

My father was a very easy-going man, very quiet. He never made demands, never asked for anything. My mother was the one with the push and the get-up-and-go. She was the one who got me into singing professionally. She had it in mind from before I was seven. She was considered one of the smart girls when she was young and she had carried on sewing professionally once she was married. In those days when you married you had to leave your job – you couldn't carry on – so she just did her dressmaking at home for people. She cared about her appearance but wasn't what you'd call glamorous nowadays. She didn't use make-up, only powder, because it wasn't done to wear make-up in those days, but she always used Pond's Cold Cream, and I used to sit on the bed and watch her put it on at the mirror at her dressing table. People called her 'nice-looking': she was pale with dark, bobbed hair, which she set herself in waves. One of my favourite photographs of her shows her wearing a black dress cinched at the waist with a silver belt buckle and she's wearing a beautiful lace collar. That's just how I like to remember her.

As a child I wasn't interested in dressing up and showing off myself. I suppose at those early house parties I was like most little girls – torn between a desire to show what I could do and shyness at the idea of standing up and singing in front of a roomful of people. Oddly enough, in time I really came to resent being asked to sing at parties and hated it when Mum would encourage her friends to call out those dreaded words 'Come on, give us a song.' And I have to confess I still hate that sort of thing; even today, if I'm at a party, I get very uncomfortable at the thought of having to get up and sing. That's why, at the sing-songs round the piano which we occasionally have at home, no matter who's there I'd never ask them to do a turn.

Besides the entertainment that the immediate family and the club could offer, there was that of the professional variety theatre. The old lady opposite my grandmother's in Ladysmith Avenue had a girl living with her as some kind of companion and this girl would sometimes take me to the East Ham Palace, where it was threepence to go up in the gods. This was our local variety theatre, right next to East Ham Station. I'd gaze down from our seats practically in the roof and dream of being on a stage like that myself one day. They had all sorts of different acts on there: comics, singers, dancers, acrobats, magicians – they weren't necessarily famous but they were professionals, all working the circuit. A comic called Wood sticks in my mind and I saw Florrie Forde there when I was about ten years old – I remember her on stage all dressed up and singing songs. She would probably have had top billing as she was a very popular Australian entertainer best known for singing, 'It's a Long Way to Tipperary' and 'Pack Up Your Troubles in Your Old Kit Bag'. She had entertained the troops during the First World War and she would perform until the day she died in 1940, straight after an engagement singing for the troops. She made a lasting impression on me.

After I started singing in public at the age of seven, my childhood changed. I tended to be working when most little girls were simply enjoying themselves. So I was not much like other little girls. Even earlier than that I was a solitary child. I don't remember having any friends before my school days, and for a long time even after I went to school I was never allowed to visit any other child's house. There was a girl in the street with whom I was friendly when I was little. That was Maudie Monshall. If I played outside, it was just outside the front door. I wasn't allowed to wander. I wasn't allowed in the street to play and it was a big privilege to be given permission to go and play in the park for an hour. I wasn't consciously aware that my mother was being strict and protective, but looking back now I think she must have been. She was nothing like so strict with my brother, Roger. Three years older than me, he seemed to go pretty much where he liked and to make whatever friends he chose; he was always off out somewhere. Not that I really minded being on my own such a lot, for just as I didn't feel at the time that my mother was being unusually firm, so I never thought about all those friends I didn't have. Certainly in those days, children never questioned their parents.

There was certainly no shortage in the immediate neighbourhood of children about my age – this was a time, remember, when large families were still not uncommon, and there were several near by, though for some reason there were far more boys than girls. One of the girls who lived opposite was a little horror called Mary, who tipped up my doll's pram and smashed the face of the doll. In those days dolls' heads were all made of china, and an accident to your favourite doll often proved fatal. I obviously took great care of the one that replaced it, for I've still got it and I'd hate anything to happen to it, because once when I young I actually used it on stage as a prop. It was dressed exactly as I was; I sang 'Glad Rag Doll', and won a prize.

Little girls seem to divide into two kinds – those who love dolls and those who don't. My own daughter, Virginia, never had any time for them – only teddy bears – but I was very much a doll person, so obviously a good deal of my solitary playing revolved round them. Luckily there was a garden at the house in Ladysmith Avenue, and as well as being a place to play, it was a plaything in itself. Strictly speaking, it was my grandmother's garden, but I had a tiny piece of it for myself, where I built a rockery. One of my ambitions was to grow up and have an enormous rockery; like the horse I was going to have one day. I still haven't got it, but I look back on that little heap of stones with great affection. I made a tiny lawn in front of it from tufts of grass weeded out of other parts of the garden, and which I used to cut with a pair of scissors. I would keep myself busy for hours in that garden.

My very close friend, Maudie, used to come and play sometimes, and we found a special use for the arched trellis that ran across the garden. With Maudie as my audience, I used to pretend I was entering a stage – through the arch, a quick bow or curtsey graciously to right and left, and into my performance. Sometimes we'd do a double act, playing to just a strip of lawn and my grandmother's gladioli. Or so we thought. I didn't discover till years later that the neighbours had been watching these antics all the time. I must have presented a strange picture – this tiny girl, gravely acknowledging imaginary applause, unconsciously preparing for the future.

At the bottom of the garden there was a shed, which seems to have been my dad's province, and I remember he would sit in it singing that music hall favourite 'I Wouldn't Leave My Little Wooden Hut For You'. In everything he did out there I would be his mate, talking to him in a special kind of dialogue we had, where he called me Jim and I called him Bill. One of the jobs he would do out there was to mend all the family's shoes on one of those three-footed iron shoe lasts you used to be able to get. He'd cut the leather and hammer away. I don't know if he held the nails in his mouth the way professional cobblers do, but I can remember him working the raw, pale buff edges of the cut leather with black heel-ball (the stiff wax used by cobblers) to get a good professional-looking finish. He had a passion for bright-green paint, so in time the dustbin, the coalbox, the doors and the window frames all ended up a vivid green. And I loved to paint pictures – and still do – so I used to pinch this paint for doing grass.

There was always a lot of grass in my paintings, but not just because I had plenty of green paint handy, nor because I was a town-bred child longing for the country. I did long for the country, but I was lucky enough to know what it was really like. This is another reason why I believe that my childhood was a little different from that of the average East Londoner in the early 1920s. For that I have to thank Auntie Maggie and the fact that she lived at a place called Weybourne. The nearest towns are Farnham and Aldershot, one on either side of the Surrey–Hampshire boundary, and they have grown now until they almost meet each other. But when I was a little girl, Weybourne, more or less halfway between the two, was not much more than a straggle of houses by a crossroads, with plenty of open country round about.

And there, every year, my mother, my brother Roger and I would spend the whole of August, with my father joining us for part of the time, staying with Auntie Maggie, Uncle George and Cousin Georgie. Those visits to Weybourne were the high point in my young life. If the steaming kettles and the illness and the tiny incidents in the flat in Thackeray Road make up my very first impressions, that's all they are – a succession of fleeting images. But my memories of those holi-days in Weybourne are among the most precious things I possess, and they have coloured the whole of my life. There is no doubt that they shaped my future: at every moment of stress or discomfort in my life, I have been able to draw on them. Years later in 1944, when I found myself in the unbe-lievable, sticky heat of Burma, I suddenly remembered the cool taste of water taken from a well near Weybourne when I was a girl. When I returned from Burma one of the first things I longed for was the English countryside, and that is exactly where I returned. It was the beginning of a lifelong love affair with the quiet rural life.

Children love ritual, and I loved every detail of the ritual of those holidays. I have a special memory which captures everything wonderful about that time: my mother, father and my Auntie Maggie are lying in a field next to a hayrick, laugh-ing their heads off. It was a time for all of us to relax and have fun. It began with the excitement on the station platform at Waterloo, and I can even recall the sense of disappointment I felt the first year that the trains were electric and not steam. The very smell and sounds of the steam train were part of knowing that the holiday had begun. The next part of the ritual was the arrival at Aldershot station and seeing my cousin's face poking through the slatted gate at the side of the platform. Then we'd set off to walk to Weybourne; sometimes it was very early in the morning, and if my uncle had been on night duty – he was some sort of lorry driver – he'd meet us at a little coffee shop near the station and help us carry our cases. It seemed a very long walk, though it couldn't have been more than about a mile, and at the end of it there was another ritual: my auntie, who was living then in part of a very old house (which has now gone), would always be watching for us over the hedge. Unpacking was another ceremony: the new plimsolls, the gingham dress made for the occasion by my mother – these were the very symbols of freedom, to be taken from the case with full understanding of their significance. It was as if the holiday couldn't start until all these little rites had been observed.

There were certain things that had to be done each year as well; otherwise the holiday wasn't complete. There was an old barn at the back of the house, with a rope we used to swing on; we would go there at the first opportunity and enjoy the creepy darkness and mustiness. (It reminded us of *Maria Marten and the Red Barn* – one of the plays I knew from the club at home about the famous murder in the 1800s of a country girl by her squire lover in a barn). When we had grown up a little and Auntie Maggie had moved into a new council house across the road, there were four walks that must be taken each holiday: up the hill to the common, along the road to Farnham one way, to Aldershot in the other direction, and down the hill for the really long trudge to Crooksbury Hill and Frensham Ponds. Frensham was all of six or seven miles away, but we thought nothing of it. At least, Mum and I and Roger didn't, but my cousin hated walking, and grumbled all the way. Frensham meant a swim and a bus most of the way back. Crooksbury Hill you can actually see from Weybourne, and when we got back from there we used to say to each other, 'Look, that's where we've been – all that way.' There were shorter walks too: of an evening across the fields, for lemonade outside the Six Bells Inn; or along the rough farm track and across a humpback bridge over the railway to where a lovely old couple called Bill and Annie Walker had a cottage with a well in the garden where we'd stop for a drink of their water.

On the whole, Weybourne didn't mean incidents so much as atmosphere; it was walks and flowers and green grass and fresh air and picnics. It was people: a real aunt and uncle, plus a crowd of friendly adults we always knew − in the fashion of the day − as aunties and uncles. It was like having a huge family in the country, and a whole circuit of houses to visit. There were the usual cuts and bruises, the quarrels and the getting into trouble, which are part of childhood, but I remember Weybourne mostly as a place of calm pleasures and small but intense excitements.

The one major excitement befell my brother Roger, not me, and happened a little later. He would have been about twelve, which would have made me nine. There was a pub called The Elm Tree, and near by a real elm, an enormous one on a crossroads. Roger was standing under this tree one day when he saw, careering towards him down the lane, a big metal army wagon with two huge bolting horses at the head of it. They appeared to be coming straight at him, so naturally he dodged round the tree, only to find when he emerged from the other side of the trunk that the runaway horses and the wagon still seemed to be heading for him. Wherever he put himself, the horses were apparently bent on getting Roger. The driver had completely lost control − in fact by this time he might well have jumped or been thrown off − so obviously the thing was lurching from side to side so much that it gave the impression of being all over the place. Roger can never remember how long he kept up this scuttling backwards and forwards around the tree, though at the time it felt like ages. But within what must in reality have been only a few seconds, the horses had rushed past him and they ended up by going through the window of the frail little shop, Mason's, where we bought our sweets. Roger was probably a bit shaken for a while, but nothing upsets you for long at twelve and afterwards it made him feel rather proud and manly. (Not long after this Roger and I became much closer – which we hadn't really been as small children – when we started ballroom dancing together in our teens. We used to practise in the clubs.)

Otherwise Roger's memories of Weybourne are not as vivid as mine. The annual visits went on until I was almost out of my teens, but I was the one who kept going back long after that – until Auntie Maggie moved right away, in fact. Throughout my childhood I always told myself that nobody could have been more miserable than I was at the end of every August. My gloom would get deeper and deeper as we came closer to Waterloo, and would reach its lowest – almost despair – on the final bus ride back to East Ham. 'Why have we got to come back to all the streets and houses? Why can't we always live in the country?' I'd ask my mother. And my mother, who always said she wouldn't want to 'shut herself away', as she called it, in some village, probably dismissed it as end-of-holiday grizzling. But I was in deadly earnest, which is why I live in the country now, in Sussex. The dream that I had as a little girl, to never have to leave the country, eventually came true for me. I realize, of course, that I'm able to live in the country because of the career I chose – or perhaps I should say because of the career that chose me – and I was deep into that even before Roger thought the horses were after him.

CHAPTER TWO

One-&-six for an Encore

People find it hard to believe that I started singing regularly in the clubs when I was seven, but there's nothing strange about it at all, really. With the club life practically in my blood, with a tradition of party singing deeply ingrained in the whole family, and with my own voice already – so I've been told – distinctive in some uncanny way, finding myself singing songs to a real audience, with just a piano for accompaniment, felt almost as natural and inevitable as growing up. I look very serious and grown-up in the photographs from the time, dressed in silk and satin dresses with ruffles which my mother designed and made herself. In one – I must be about seven – I am dressed as a fairy wearing a dress with a sequinned bodice and have a huge net skirt!

The costumes, along with everything else in my early career, were largely down to my mother's influence: she wanted me to perform. I have to say now that I didn't particularly enjoy singing. The idea came from the family – it certainly didn't come from me. For me it was a case of 'Don't put your daughter on the stage, Mrs Worthington'. But I had no choice. It was my mother who saw that I started doing formal concerts. And, to my amazement, I got paid for it, although obviously I didn't see the money myself.

It didn't happen entirely automatically, of course; somebody had to provide the first push. That came from a man named Pat Barry, who was a male 'soubrette' on the working men's club circuit. 'Soubrette' is an odd kind of word, but it used to be bandied about in the business. Originally it meant a girl who sang and danced. By the time the concert parties and then the revues had come along, the word had taken on the meaning of a young female member of the cast who could sing and dance and act, and was therefore useful in several ways. Pat Barry's talents were singing and tap dancing and clog dancing. A sort of jack-of-all-trades for the stage, then.

Pat knew the family, he'd heard me sing at parties and he thought that I was good enough to appear as an act; and he not only persuaded my mother and father that I ought to go on, but – being an all-rounder himself and keen on the idea of having at least a second accomplishment to call on – he told me I ought to learn to step dance as well. So once a week round at his house he'd teach me to dance on a proper little slatted step-dancing mat on the kitchen floor – a roll-up mat of wooden slats on straps that your shoes would 'clack' against. I was tall and leggy as a child and, although that first big illness seemed to have left me unable to run far without getting out of breath, I was acrobatic and nimble enough, and did pretty well. But for me, singing – with all the appropriate actions – was to be the main thing, and the club would bill me as a 'descriptive child vocalist'.

The clubs themselves were part of a network of entertainment of which, unless you grew up in it, you could be completely unaware. There have been working men's clubs in practically every industrial and thickly populated working-class area since the end of the nineteenth century, and the East London clubs I started in were just a few out of literally hundreds of such places. The old Mildmay Club at Newington Green was one of the best known.

I appeared many times at the Mildmay, with its large hall where the rows of chairs had ledges on the backs of them to hold glasses of beer, and where the chairman and committee of the club sat in front of the stage at a long table. That was the standard practice and, very much as in an old-fashioned music hall, the chairman could quickly gauge the mood of an audience. This was very important, because it was the committee who decided, according to the strength of the applause, whether you were worth an encore or not. That made all the difference to the money you earned: an extra encore earned you a shilling and sixpence. An encore also meant you were well in, and if it happened in a club you were new to, you could be sure that the entertainments secretary would have taken note of how you went down and would book you again.

In the working men's clubs the entertainments secretaries were roughly the equivalent of agents, and like agents they were always visiting other clubs, on the look-out for new acts. They were unpaid, but every so often the club would run a benefit night for its entertainments secretary. These were known as 'nanty' jobs (the word comes from *niente*, Italian for 'nothing'), because the performers offered their services free. Artists would try hard to appear on these shows, for apart from anything else, they were the accepted way of getting into a new club. If you could do a nanty job for an entertainments secretary who didn't know your act, then it worked like an audition. If he liked you, you'd go down in his book of contacts and you could expect him to remember you later for a paid performance.

Some artists remained more or less permanent fixtures on the club circuit; others used the clubs as a way into 'the business' and a step towards bigger things. The comedy team of Bennett and Williams began in the clubs as a double act known, if I remember rightly, as Prop and Cop; the comedian and actor Max Wall started in the clubs too. The Beverley Sisters' parents were a club act called The Corams. These were names and faces from the bills I used to appear on as a child.

For my first appearance, when Pat Barry got an entertainments secretary to put me on, I learned three songs and had a new dress made: white lace with little mauve bows – I can see it now. You didn't have 'dresses' in those days; you had one dress and that was it. (When that one got shabby, if you were lucky you got another one.) I had a pair of silver pumps, a tiny briefcase from Woolworth's for sixpence and my rolled-up music, and off I went. Later I would suffer from nerves, like everybody else, but at seven I was simply too young to feel anxious. The thing that excited me was the medal I'd been promised for going on. Our next-door neighbour in Ladysmith Avenue was Charlie Paynter, the trainer/manager of West

Ham United football team, and he had said he'd give me a West Ham United medallion if I sang in public. He kept his promise, and I was thrilled, because he was a very important man in our locality. My parents would have been with me that first time too, but I don't remember them telling me that I'd done well or anything like that. I just remember not wanting to do it but knowing that I had to. The applause made me feel good, though, and I got an encore – and got paid for that.

I don't remember what I sang on that first occasion, but I know that from my earliest days I seemed to be attracted naturally to the straightforward sentimental ballad. In spite of – or maybe, come to think of it, because of – the happy times I had with my dad, I practically cornered the market in 'daddy' numbers: 'Dream Daddy'; 'I've Got a Real Daddy Now'; and a genuine 22-carat tear-jerker called 'What is a Mammy, Daddy?' I sang that at a competition once:

> *What is a mammy, daddy?*
> *Everyone's got one but me,*
> *Is she the lady what lives next door*
> *Who cooks our dinner and sweeps up the floor?*
> *I've got no mammy to put me to bed*
> *And tell me to go out to play.*
> *Daddy I'll be such a very good girl,*
> *If you'll bring me a mammy some day.*

Everybody was in tears, and there was tremendous applause, but I didn't win. When the results were announced, the audience kept shouting out, 'What about the little girl in the red dress?' and, in the end, I got a consolation prize. This particular competition took place not far from home in Poplar, East London, and it was one of a whole series run at various cinemas in London by Nat Travers, a local cockney comedian. Afterwards he came round to me and my mum and said, 'Sorry about that, ducks, but come to Tottenham Court Road next week. I've got another competition on there and you'll be all right.' But my mother was furious and wouldn't let me go in for any more of his contests.

Remembering a song, once I've learned it, has never been a problem for me, and I could still probably sing you an hour and a half's worth straight off without repeating myself. I've always been able to decide quickly *how* to sing a song – how to phrase it, what to emphasize. But I had enormous difficulty in learning the words in the first place. I would sit on the floor at home for hours on end, going over them again and again, while my mother doggedly picked out the tune on the piano. Often there'd be tears, and even when I'd finally managed to get a song into my head and came to sing it in public for the first time I'd be petrified in case I forgot the words. Ever so many times I wished I could give the whole thing up, just for this one reason.

Finding material was comparatively easy. The writing and publishing and selling of popular songs was a business then just as it is now, but it was a different kind of business. Live public performances were what counted, not the plugging of records, and anybody who was known to appear regularly in front of an audience could count on being welcome at the various music publishers' offices, which were then nearly all in

Denmark Street, just off Charing Cross Road, the British 'Tin Pan Alley'. This was where all the music publishers were based, and if they knew you could put a song over, they were often willing to give you copies. So, from quite an early age, I was a familiar little figure up there – something which was to stand me in good stead later when I started broadcasting.

That 'descriptive child vocalist' billing was no mere gimmick. Even when I was very small I had an unusual voice, loud, penetrating, and rather low in pitch for my age; most songs had to be transposed from their original key into something more suitable. When I became better known, the publishers would usually do that themselves, but at first I always had to go to someone outside. We found a Mr Winter-bottom, who would do you a 'right-hand part' for sixpence a copy; if you wanted a left-hand as well it came to one-and-six, but we just used to have the top line done because most of the club pianists were so experienced at this kind of work – which was more than a cut above the 'you-whistle-it-and-I'll-follow-you' school – that was all they needed.

You'd merely hand your music over and they would improvise a bass part on the spot. One or two were actually publishers' pianists by day – the men whose job was to demonstrate songs to prospective professional customers. (All that has gone now, but forty and fifty years ago that was the accepted way of selling a performer a new number, and those pianists could transpose anything into any key, at sight.) Every now and again you would come across a club pianist who wasn't much good, but they must have been in a minority, because I can't recall any great musical disasters.

One minor catastrophe was not the pianist's fault but mine. Without being a typical 'stage mother', my mum always took a very close interest in every aspect of my singing, and my programme for any given appearance was usually the result of a kind of joint decision. We didn't disagree often, but there was one night when I very much wanted to do one song, and she thought I ought to do another. I must have been a stubborn child, for in the end I won, and it was decided I would sing the one I wanted. I gave the pianist the music for it, but the moment he'd rattled through an introduction (and I must say club pianists' introductions could sound pretty much alike), I immediately began singing the other one. For a few disorganized bars the two numbers tangled with each other; we both stopped and started, like two people trying to pass one another but always ending up in each other's way. We did the only thing we could do, and began again from the top. Audiences don't dislike this sort of thing as much as some artists believe; as long as it doesn't happen too often, there's something strangely reassuring about seeing somebody else make a mistake.

That much I accept, and could accept even then. What I couldn't take were the efforts of some well-meaning entertainments secretaries who would see my deadpan little face and urge me to 'Smile, dear – smile'. I'd come back at them with, 'I'm not going to smile; I'm singing a sad song' – and I usually was – 'so why should I have to grin all over my face?'

I was aware that I did not have much choice but to go on stage. Money was short in those days, so any money I could earn helped to swell the household coffers. I hardly ever wanted to be at these concerts, though, and later I was always nervous before I went on. Nobody asked me if I wanted to sing or not. You didn't argue in those days; you did as you were told. That makes me laugh now, when I think of how youngsters are today. It never entered my mind to be angry with my mother, but there were times when I wasn't happy. I don't ever remember saying the words, 'I don't want to do it and I'm not going to,' which is what kids of today might do. This went on until I was about fifteen or sixteen – it wasn't until I started singing with bands that I started to enjoy it more.

I did club work for something like eight years, mostly in east and north London and on the Essex fringe, but also over the river in places like Woolwich and Plumstead, which were comparatively easy to get to because of the Blackwall tunnel. Coming back from Woolwich one night we missed a bus and had to walk all the way through the tunnel, which had only a tiny pavement and wasn't really designed for pedestrians, to pick up the tram at Poplar. And there were many other nights when I would wait at Poplar in the cold and wet, and being so tired that I'd fall asleep on the bus long before we got home. While I was still small enough, my dad would sometimes give me a piggyback home late at night, and it was wonderful to stop on the way for fish and chips and what we used to call wally-wallies, which were big dill pickles. Occasionally on the way to a club, when the shops were still open, we'd call in at the little grocer's near the end of the road for a penn'orth of broken biscuits. These were a great bargain because biscuits came in big square tins in those days and were bought loose –

any that got broken were sold off cheap, even the most expensive ones.

Nowadays if child performers earn any money the parents are able to build up the child's bank account and put money aside for their future. But in my day they were only too glad of the money to keep the house going. Although my father had a job, when I started earning money that helped pay the food bills. In fact the money I earned more than fed me. If I had concerts on the weekend and a cabaret somewhere I could earn seven shillings and sixpence. Unless I did two places in one night, which I did regularly: then I could earn more. And if the public wanted an encore, then the men sitting around the committee table in the club would put money in a kitty – up to one shilling and six. That was useful because it paid for our fares, either on a sixpenny tram or on a shilling-all-night tram. In those days my dad was probably earning about three pounds fifty a week. So there were some weekends when I could almost make in two nights what my father made in a week.

I was not allowed to spend any of the money I earned myself. I didn't feel good or bad about it; I didn't think about it. I just did the concerts, knowing that whatever money I earned, it would go into the household. In my younger days going to school I would be given a penny to buy a chocolate cupcake from the bakery opposite the school, and I would have that in my break. It was a little spongey cake with chocolate melted on top, which used to go all hard and crispy – it was so nice. As long as I had my penny for the school break, I never thought to ask for anything more than that.

I knew that the money made a big difference to the family as it was a lot of money in those days. You don't analyse these things when you're young, but we were always well fed, although not by today's standards, maybe. The children of today just help themselves to whatever they want. You weren't allowed to help yourself back then – we would have eaten at mealtimes but rarely between. The only time we had a bowl of oranges on the side was at Christmas. The rest of the year fruit was kept in the larder. I didn't consider our family poor, though: we were just middle of the road. We never really went short of anything.

I was certainly never hungry. My mother was a plain cook but a good cook. Most women were in those days. There wasn't all the fancy cooking that we do today. It was basic. We had a roast every Sunday – Mother used to make very good Yorkshire pudding – and then the cold meat on the Monday. And we always had two different sorts of potatoes: roast and boiled. I was thinking about that the other day when I was peeling potatoes: that at home on Sundays there was always a choice. They don't do that nowadays, do they? You get either boiled or roast, but not both. Funny how things change.

All this time, of course, I was at school, and although the work I did in the clubs was mostly at weekends, the two things still managed to clash – sometimes in unexpected ways. At my junior school in Central Park Road I once asked if I could borrow a copy of the sheet music of 'Your Land and My Land', and when I told the teacher what I wanted it for she said, 'Oh, you sing, do you?' Obviously she remembered, because one morning at assembly not long after that I was suddenly called on to sing this song. I was petrified, and I had every reason to be, for as I've mentioned, my voice was of a rather unorthodox pitch for a little girl, so when the school played it from the original song copy, it was in completely the wrong key for me. It was a terrible mess, and although it wasn't my fault I was crimson with shame. They must have thought, Good God! How can this child go on stage and sing!

As a matter of fact everything we sang at school was pitched too high for me. Most of the time I couldn't get up there, and the only alternative was to go into a kind of falsetto voice, which was disastrous. The school disliked my singing voice so much that ironically I was only allowed in the front row of the choir because I opened my mouth nice and wide and it looked good.

If I was ever tired at school it was automatically put down to my going out singing late at night 'in those terrible places'. My voice and the sort of singing I was doing were much looked down on. One teacher in particular was most unsympathetic. One day she wouldn't let me go home early in time to get to a competition at East Ham Granada, so when we did come out of school I had to run all the way home, where my mother was waiting with my things – this was the time I sang with my doll – and then we both ran all the way there. I wasn't much of a runner, and I arrived out of breath, just as the last competitor was coming off. I flew on, somehow struggled through my number – 'A Glad Rag Doll' – and won first prize. Ten bob, it was, and it bought me and my mum enough of that red ripply material that everybody used for dressing gowns in those days to make us a dressing gown each.

I was never keen on school – probably because I wasn't good at any of the academic subjects. I could never spell; I couldn't add up; I couldn't assimilate the facts in history and geography. I never tried very hard at French; I didn't need French, I was going to be a singer – I can actually remember thinking that. How foolish can you be? I've bitterly regretted my poor record at that kind of subject ever since, and it's left me with a permanent sense of inferiority in certain kinds of company. As if in compensation, I was always good at anything with my hands – drawing, painting and sewing. Gardening too, even then; when we made a crazy paving path at my secondary school, Brampton Road School, I took charge of laying out the pieces. Maybe it's still there. Cookery was something else I was good at, and botany, though my marks in that came mostly from my little sketches. I wasn't a great reader, but I read quite well out loud in class – I suppose there was some kinship there with projecting a song. I tended to be good at what came easily to me, and made heavy weather of everything else, like learning songs. But I just wasn't academic. In fact I never learned to read music, not even to this day.

The whole act of going to school was rather like learning new words, as a matter of fact, because no matter how much I may have disliked it, I never tried to get out of it; I knew it had to be done. I suffered a great deal from bilious attacks as a child, but even if I'd been up nearly all night and felt like death the next morning, when my mother would ask me if I wanted to stay at home, I'd have to explain that I had to go – I musn't miss school. It turned out in later life that one of the things that was causing the biliousness, and the being ill after eating, say, strawberries, was a troublesome appendix, which would eventually catch up with me right on the stage of the Palladium during the Blitz. But at the time I was just another of those bilious children, with maybe that difference – that instead of using the weakness as an excuse for taking it easy, I felt I had actively to fight it. If I'm not doing what I'm supposed to be doing, I feel I'm slacking. I've got to *deserve* a rest; I feel each day that I've got to *earn* my day. My mother was the same, never still. She didn't slow down until the mid-1970s, when infirmity forced her to (she died not many years after that), and my recollection of her during my childhood is that she was always rushing about. She wanted to get a lot done, and I suppose I do, too.

We shared that practical streak. As mentioned already, my mother had been a dressmaker before I was born, and not only made all my dresses and costumes during those early years but, when the Depression came and my dad was out of work for a spell, went back to dressmaking rather more seriously in order to help out, and I suppose my seven-and-sixes must have been quite a help.

When I was eleven the pattern of my young career changed a little. I still carried on with the solo club singing, but I also joined a juvenile troupe with the ringing title of Madame Harris's Kracker Kabaret Kids, and that was when, for professional purposes, I changed my name.

I never doubted that I was going to be a singer, and the instinct that had prompted me, when I was very tiny, to sing 'Dream Daddy' and follow it up with 'I've Got a Real Daddy Now' suggested that I ought to adopt a more comfortable –

and more glamorous – stage name than Vera Welch. The main concern was to find something that was short and easily remembered, and that would stand out on a bill – something that would allow for plenty of space round each letter. We held a kind of family conference about it, and we found the answer within the family too. My grandmother's maiden name had been Lynn; it seemed to be everything a stage name ought to be, but at the same time it was a real one. From then on, I was to be Vera Lynn.

In spite of its exotic name, Madame Harris's Kracker Kabaret Kids was run from a house in Central Park Road, East Ham. As a juvenile troupe it prospered, and it quickly outgrew Madame Harris's front parlour and transferred its activities, every Saturday morning, to the local Salvation Army hut; we used to pay sixpence each towards the cost of hiring it. I don't know exactly how Madame Harris advertised the tuition she offered, but it's my guess that she must have been an early exponent of 'Ballet, Tap and Acro.', that faintly ridiculous-sounding description you used to see on local advertising boards and among the small ads in local papers. Acrobatic I certainly was, with my long legs and my ability to kick high; while Pat Barry's wisdom in insisting on my doing some tap dancing meant that I was halfway there as far as dancing was concerned. After a while I used to teach the kids while Madame Harris banged away at the piano. In fact it became something of a family concern, for my mother and Mrs Harris, between them, made all the costumes for our shows.

The troupe was a very busy performing unit, working the clubs as I had always done, but going rather farther afield, usually travelling in a small coach. On a trip to Dagenham once the driver got it into his head that he had to get us there in a great hurry, and drove like a madman all the way. We were terrified, and I seem to remember that we spent most of the journey screaming. He must have been driving very badly, because on the whole children are only aware of that kind of danger when it gets physically alarming, and I have a very clear recollection of being pitched all over the place. When you consider how much higher off the ground all the cars and buses were in those days, you can understand our certain belief that we were going to turn over. How we managed to dance and sing properly at the end of it I can't think.

The other trip that sticks in my mind was part of what turned out in the end to be a rather longer stay away from home. It must have been during the Christmas holidays one year, because we'd been booked to do three nights in pantomime at – wait for it – the Corn Exchange, Leighton Buzzard. I don't know whether the extra distance was a strain on the Kracker Kids' finances, or whether the coach contractor was out of favour after the Dagenham Grand Prix run, or what, but this time we'd hired a vegetable van, with a flap at the back, to take us to and from the engagement. The arrangement lasted one night only. You know that old tag line 'We had one but the wheel came off'? Well, it did, somewhere out on the edge of London where the tramlines ended. We were on the way home in the small hours of the morning when one of the wheels of this van came off, and there we were, a bunch of kids and a few mums stranded in a freezing street in some unfamiliar suburb. Keeping ourselves warm was the main problem, and we ran up and down for what seemed like hours, trying to keep our circulations going while we waited for the first tram to come along.

Eventually we got home at about six in the morning, though God knows what sort of state we were in, and we somehow went back to Leighton Buzzard the next night. But Mrs Harris decided we weren't going to take any more risks and she found somewhere for us to stay for those two nights. All I can remember of our dubious accommodation is that we had to go up a winding staircase and all the girls were put in one room, the boys in another and the mums somewhere else, and in the middle of everything my mother was wandering about with a spoon in one hand and a bottle of syrup of figs in the other, dosing us one by one. This was in the heyday of parental belief in laxatives, of course, and what with that and the candles we had to carry to find our way to the loo it was like something out of *Oliver Twist*. Now I stop to think about it, the Leighton Buzzard Corn Exchange itself must have been pretty Dickensian, because all the backstage passages were unlit, and we had to use candles to find our way around the rambling passages. That must have been the first occasion when entertaining other people caused me to spend a night away from home. I couldn't possibly have guessed then that eventually I should lose count of the times that happened, and that for part of my life that would be the rule rather than the exception.

I'm sure I was too busy concentrating on the job in hand to think of things like that, and in any case I always took my career a step at a time. It was very much a matter of steps then, too, for with one or two exceptions we were a strong dancing team. Which doesn't mean we were short of soloists. Apart from myself there was Leslie, a boy soprano, who eventually made some records as Leslie Day, 'the 14-year-old Wonder Voice Boy Soprano – Sings with the Perfect Art of a Coloratura Soprano'. My cousin Joan was in the troupe, too. Where I was tall and thin, she was short and tubby. She didn't go on with it after the troupe days ended – she was my mother's sister's daughter, and had been rather pushed into it – but she had a terrific voice, and used to sing meaty songs like 'The Trumpeter'. Unfortunately, she couldn't dance to save her life. We used to try to teach her, but she'd just clop from foot to foot, saying, 'I hate this, I hate it.' Another boy, Bobby, who was a future Battle of Britain pilot, was a kind of juvenile lead, and we had little Dot, Bobby's sister, who was tiny and sang Florrie Forde numbers and one or two Marie Lloyd songs, like 'My Old Man Said Follow the Van'. Eileen Fields was another soubrette type. She and I would do duets occasionally – we dressed up as an old couple for one of them and sang 'My Old Dutch'. Mrs Harris's daughter, Doreen, was a good singer too, and in fact she practically ran the troupe; later on she became the wife of Leon Cortez, an actor who went on to appear in *Dixon of Dock Green*, *The Saint* and *Dad's Army* in the 1960s. Doreen and I were the ones who went on into the profession itself, and when Doreen left to start broadcasting Mrs Harris asked me to take over instead. Soon after that, Mrs Harris packed it in altogether, and I took over the school for a year until I, too, got involved in other things.

I was with the troupe for about four years, and had a lot of fun. Some of the children clearly had no liking for it and no talent, and had merely been conscripted into it by ambitious mothers, but on the whole I don't think we can have been too bad. We certainly did plenty of work, especially during the school holidays, when we often did shows on the stages of the big local cinemas. As juveniles we were subject to fairly strict controls and licensing regulations; you had to be over fourteen to appear on public stages after a certain hour at night without a licence, which ruined our chances when cousin Joan and I went in for a competition once. We were both under age and neither of us had a licence, but we got through to the semi-final without anyone bothering to check up. Then they said, 'When you come tomorrow you'll have to bring your birth certificate with you,' but they said it to Joan and not to me. They never said it to me because I looked fourteen, even though I wasn't. But they wanted Joan's birth certificate, and that would have given the show away. We tried for hours to work out some way round it, but in the end we had to admit defeat, so that was us out of the competition, even though we felt we had a good chance of winning.

I don't suppose 'That's show business' had become a common phrase by that time, but presumably I accepted that setback (if that's what it was) as simply one obstacle which time would remove. For in due course I would be fourteen and such problems wouldn't arise.

I would also be free to leave school. Fourteen was the official leaving age, though you could stay on another year if you wanted to. The drama teacher begged me not to leave, because she wanted to put me into all sorts of productions, but all I wanted was to get away from school. Once I'd left, of course, I began wanting to go back. I realized I'd wasted a lot of precious time by not concentrating; I felt ignorant, and I wanted to return and make up for it.

Not that I ever doubted for a moment that I was going to be a professional singer. Judging by the way she stood over me while I learned my songs, by the way she helped with my costumes and by the way she came with me to whatever show I was doing, whichever club I was working at, I don't think my mother could have doubted it either. But when I left school she wavered, offering the classic and very reasonable objection that there wasn't enough security in the life of a professional popular singer. Actually her plan seemed not to have been for me to work at all in the ordinary sense, but to stay at home and help her while carrying on as usual – only more actively – in the clubs. In other words I was to continue to do as much singing as I could get, but that I wasn't to regard it as my profession.

I didn't fancy that, because the girl next door had stayed at home after she left school, and in no time at all she seemed to have turned into an old maid. I didn't want to be like that, so I decided I ought to have a job and I went and signed on at the Labour Exchange. It took them six weeks to come up with something, by which time I'd already lost any enthusiasm for the idea before I even went to a little factory at East Ham to start sewing on buttons for a living. I sat down with a number of other young girls, but we weren't even allowed to talk. When lunchtime came I went into a little back room with my sandwiches and felt thoroughly miserable. The day seemed never ending.

When I finally did get home, my dad asked me how I'd got on.

'Horrible,' I said. 'You must do this and you mustn't do that. I don't want to go back there any more.'

'How much do you get?' he asked.

'Six-and-six.'

'A day?'

'No, for the week.'

'Be damned to that,' he said. 'Why, you can earn more than that for one concert. You're not going back there. What do you have to put up with it all for?'

So I never did go back, and I got a postal order for one-and-a-penny for my day's work. I can't say that at this stage I really had any idea myself what I wanted to do with my life. Children thought differently in those days to how they think today. Now they have ideas of what they want to do, but in those days you just went along with what your mother or father said.

But it was fairly typical of my father to side with me over the button factory. He was very much the one for going along with the wishes of his children. In fact he was an enormously easy-going man altogether. While my mother was the sort who, for some years to come, would wait up for me after a show so that I dare not linger or go to any of the many parties that were held, Dad would have said, 'Go on, mate, do as you like, mate; enjoy yourself, I'm going off to bed.' Only two things ever really seemed to upset him, and they were quite trivial. If you gave him a cup of tea that hadn't been sugared he'd carry on as if you'd tried to poison him; and he hated being expected to go to tea at anybody else's home.

It was the strong principles of my mother that laid down the rules that gave our household and my childhood their peculiar flavour. For example, most families at that time, no matter what their religious views, tended to encourage the children to go to Sunday school, if only to get them out of the way for an hour or so on a Sunday. We were positively not allowed to go to Sunday school. My mother didn't think it was right to go to church or Sunday school during the day on Sunday, and then go singing in the clubs on Sunday night. I think she was wrong, but that's what she believed, and there seemed nothing strange about it at the time.

At the latter end of my period with Mrs Harris's juvenile troupe I was starting to work quite hard as a young entertainer. By the time I left school at fourteen I had, to all intents and purposes, already been earning my living as a performer for seven years, and after that one day's orthodox employment I never thought of doing anything else. I more or less ran the troupe, and I sang and danced with it, but I still went out solo as well. The engagements were mainly club dates, as they had always been, but I was beginning to add slightly more sophisticated cabaret bookings to my diary – private social functions and dinners. On a ticket to one of them I suddenly found I was being described as 'the girl with the different voice'. That was a label I should hold on to, I realized. It was nothing spectacular, but it was progress, a kind of hint that I wasn't to remain working round the clubs for ever, and that I could expect in time to move on to something else.

That something else was to start when I was fifteen, and doing a cabaret spot at Poplar Baths. It was a nerve-racking evening when everything happened at once: I had a foul cold, I encountered my first microphone and I was heard by Howard Baker, the king of the local bandleaders. I didn't know it at the time, but it was the moment my life really took off.

CHAPTER THREE

Vocal Chorus

You can get a real flavour of the period from the advertisements and Howard Baker's ads were hardly humble:

HOWARD BAKER BANDS
– The Gig King –

Definitely the largest band organization in the country. Howard Baker Bands supplied. Also leading agents for outside combinations. We also supply first-class cabaret and concert artistes for all functions.

Nowadays wording like that has a faintly preposterous ring about it. But in the early 1930s, celebrity was infinitely graded, and while Howard Baker was not a household name, like Roy Fox or Lew Stone or Jack Payne (all bandleaders in their heyday in the 1930s), and he isn't familiar to later generations, he was every bit as successful as he implied in those pompous ads. Nobody disputed his claim to be the Gig King.

The word 'gig' in those days nearly always meant just a one-night engagement. Musicians today seem to talk of almost any kind of job as a gig, even a long residency somewhere or a complete tour. But then 'gigging around' in essence meant doing musical odd jobs. It wasn't anything like as lowly as it sounds, because back then in the 1930s, long before disco had been heard of and jukeboxes were still a rarity, the demand for live musical entertainment was tremendous and musicians would be booked to appear at anything from twenty-first birthday parties through weddings and firms' dinners to large private and public dances – 'all functions', just as the advert said.

Howard Baker began as a cornet and trumpet player, and found that he got so much work in the early twenties that he had to farm some of it out, so he set up an agency to supply bands to this greedy market. On a really busy night there could be anything up to a couple of dozen Howard Baker bands – in addition to the one he ran himself – keeping his name before the foxtrotting couples. Some of his bands went quite far afield, but since he was based in Ilford, his greatest fame was in the London area and the Thames-side Essex towns; as provider of the music for a function in Poplar, he was the obvious choice.

This meant that he and I were working the same patch. The clubs I worked at regularly, except for the ones on the Woolwich side of the river, lay within an area drawn between, say, Dagenham and Finsbury Park. Since I had some minor local fame in those parts, it's quite possible that Howard Baker wasn't unaware of me before the evening when he actually made a point of listening to me.

Poplar Baths doesn't sound a particularly promising place for furthering a career – it was a bath house that was used for concerts and events in the winter months. I was booked to appear there in the cabaret spot at some social gathering or other, and the dance music was being provided by Howard Baker. Considering how important the occasion turned out to be, it seems awful to say now that I can't remember who arranged it, but somebody had persuaded him to hear my act, so that while I was working I was doing a kind of audition. I knew in advance, because I remember being in tears over the fact that this was my big chance and I'd only gone and caught the most dreadful cold. And my colds really were distressing – still are, as a matter of fact – because that bout of diphtheric croup seemed to have left my bronchial tubes with a permanent coat of rust on them; at least, that's what it feels like whenever I catch a cold. But I told myself that I'd got to go, and do my best. I suppose it's adrenalin that sees you through situations like that, because cold or no cold, he seemed satisfied.

The microphone was another unexpected problem. Microphones weren't in general use then, and this was the first time I'd ever had to work with one. I can see it now: I walked on to the stage and there was this thing, and at first I stood well back from it. It was then that I realized that if I were to use a microphone, I was going to have to start learning an entirely different technique. I had to find out how to employ it as an instrument, and make it work for me. I can't have adapted myself too badly that night, for I went down well with the audience and Howard Baker took me on as vocalist with the band!

That brought about several changes right away, not the least of which was that I was now worth ten shillings an appearance. There was a great deal of learning and unlearning to be done. As a child performer – almost a novelty – I had literally acted out my songs dramatically (because I was sometimes billed as a 'descriptive child vocalist' I often did the full 'Shepherd of the Hills' gesticulating bit) and I had to unlearn all that. I was part of a band, and apart from the new experience of having to blend my voice with a whole lot of other instruments, it meant that while I was singing I had to stand still. Holding the microphone with one hand was a big help in that; but there was another convention of the period which made it easier than it might have been. You can imagine that a band playing all the popular tunes of the day was constantly adding new stuff to its book. With my dreadful slowness at learning an unfamiliar lyric, that would have been agony for me. But strangely enough, nobody minded seeing a vocalist standing there clutching a song sheet in those days, which not only helped me over the words problem but gave me something to do with my hands. When I wasn't singing, of course, I had to sit or stand politely to one side.

It was the microphone itself, however, that was the revelation. I'd sung in some big places without one – none of our cinema gigs with the juvenile troupe, for instance, had ever involved a microphone – and had developed a pretty piercing sort of delivery. I learned very quickly to lower my volume, but I found out at the same time that that also meant lowering the pitch: as I reduced the pressure on my voice, so it simply dropped into a lower key. I was suddenly faced with a whole set of new keys to deal with.

I suppose I was young enough not to be consciously bothered by it all, for I didn't seem to have any real difficulty in adapting myself to the needs of band singing. I'm sure there must have been some awkward moments, because having adjusted my approach to compensate for the microphone, I would still run into venues where there wasn't one. In fact, with Howard Baker at the old Holborn Restaurant one night, I actually used a megaphone, which was a bit of a giggle, since I'd only ever seen one in a film – probably wielded by Rudy Vallée, an American singer and bandleader I loved. Using a megaphone is a very strange sensation, because while you're having to sing your sentimental words, you know all the time that you look more like a rowing coach than a singer. It was all good training, and I'm especially glad that I had to discover for myself so early on what a microphone could do. For many years people complemented me on the way I used a microphone and I'm sure it's because of what I learned back then.

As far as the public and the press were concerned, I wasn't a singer though, I was a crooner. Anybody who sang with a dance band in the thirties was a crooner (soon they would even invent the word 'croonette', for there was no such thing as unisex in those days) and when I came to qualify for my first press cutting, towards the end of 1934, it was headed, with a great flourish, 'STAR IN THE EAST – East Ham's Latest Contribution to Crooning'. The crooner's status was rather ambiguous, because while it was clear that no band could afford to be without one of each gender, band singers as a whole were treated very condescendingly by most of the press. 'To many people "crooning" has become an insidious word relative to immediate action in switching off the wireless, walking out of the cinema or smashing up the gramophone,' the *East Ham Echo* said at one point in the piece about me. Admittedly it found me 'not guilty' of whatever it was that people found so objectionable about crooners, but the fact that the remark was there at all, in an otherwise complimentary article, suggests that the poor crooner was the current whipping boy or girl and was probably held responsible for the country going to the dogs.

I'd been singing with Howard Baker's various bands for close on two years when that piece appeared, and he'd kept me very busy indeed. I still did the occasional solo date, but I was getting most of my work from him. He had enough bands out at any given time for it to be possible sometimes to do more than one appearance for him in the course of an evening, and I would get ten shillings for each.

With work coming in at that rate it made sense to have a telephone put in the house, which was a big thing in those days. It was one of those old-fashioned telephones with two parts, one for your ear and one to speak into. It had the dial on the base and it was black. When you picked up the phone to make a call, you spoke directly to the operator and gave them your number. Ours started with Grosvenor and then a four-digit number. Having a phone was very exciting, and for some reason we had it in the front parlour, by the fireplace. (Actually, that wasn't such a bad idea, now I come to think of it. Next to the bathroom, if you had one – we didn't – the coldest place in an English house in those days was the hall, yet the telephone was always stuck out there among the hats and coats.) It was decidedly a necessity and not a luxury, for Howard would often call me at very short notice to go and sing with one of his bands somewhere, and soon I couldn't have got along without it. Grangewood 380-something, the number was, and it's sad to think that those pretty exchange names have gone now, and been replaced with these long numbers which are impossible to remember.

So it was that I got a call which gave me a week and a half with Billy Cotton and, with it, my first taste of the big time. A one-time amateur footballer for Brentford FC, Cotton became a well-known bandleader in the 1920s and went on to be a television personality in the 1950s. Back in the thirties Howard Baker had some kind of business tie-up with Billy Cotton on the agency side, and I believe that some of the members of the Baker bands would occasionally 'move up' into Billy Cotton's band. I got the impression that Billy Cotton had never been terribly keen on girl vocalists, but I suppose he thought he'd try one again, and he'd heard about me through Howard Baker, so I went to some bleak audition room and sang for him. He used the customary formula 'I'll let you know', and I went home not really expecting to hear any more about it. But he phoned, and said would I go to Manchester – just like that – and he'd give me five pounds for the week.

In the 1930s there was always some magic about the figure of five pounds. If you ever heard an adult say of another, 'He's getting five pounds a week,' you knew that this person had made it. But more important than that, it looked like a big step up in my career. Mum had to come with me, of course, since I was only sixteen going on seventeen – as the song says

– and that meant she had to flap round and organize someone to look after Dad at short notice. I played a week of Mecca ballrooms in the Manchester area, and the most memorable thing about the whole trip was not singing with the band but the awful place where we had digs. My only other experience of staying away from home on a job had been those two nights of candles and syrup of figs at Leighton Buzzard. This was worse – a tiny room, with one bed in it, which my mother and I shared. When we came home from the show each night there was an awful greasy supper of fish and chips or sausages waiting for us, and a great roaring coal fire halfway up the chimney, making the room so hot you could hardly breathe. If they didn't manage to poison us there was always a strong chance we'd choke to death; they seemed determined to get us one way or the other.

The following week Billy Cotton took me on to Sheffield, where the band had a week's engagement at a theatre, but this time I only lasted three days. I've never been absolutely certain what went wrong. It certainly wasn't what or how I sang, because I seemed to be very well received. I think the trouble arose because he would announce me as a little girl he'd more or less discovered, who was getting her first chance, and then I would come out full of the bounce and confidence and technique of many years' experience. He used to get furious: 'You're supposed to be an amateur,' he'd say, 'not a seasoned professional!' I'd come back at him: 'I can't help that; I can't undo everything I've taught myself. I've been doing it for nearly ten years.' That may have been the reason, although I also got the impression that he just didn't want to be bothered with having a young girl in among his hard-bitten musicians – the Billy Cotton Band of those days was always a pretty wild bunch. Anyway, he sent me home in the middle of the week. Though he did have the grace to say a few years later that it was the worst day's work he'd ever done.

So it was back to Howard Baker. I don't think I felt too badly about it. The digs in Manchester had been ghastly, and I'd learned that theatre dressing rooms could be considerably more squalid than the modest but adequate accommodation in the clubs. But going out with a nationally known band, appearing before large audiences to whom I was a total stranger, had been good experience for me. I'd always taken everything a step at a time, and if this particular step hadn't led very far, well, that was to be expected once in a while.

The next step I tried to take didn't lead anywhere at all. I was working in some club in East London, and a couple of boys who had an act said to my mother, 'Why don't you take this girl up to the BBC?' We didn't do anything about it right away, but eventually we wrote to them for an audition. The result was that I went along and sang for Henry Hall, who was doing very well in charge of the BBC Dance Orchestra – Hall was the bandleader who recorded the delightful 'Teddy Bears' Picnic' with the BBC Dance Orchestra in 1932. He turned me down. Many years later he used to say that it was because my voice was not one that would have blended with his music. Whatever it was, he considered me unsuitable. I must have been disappointed, but no matter, there was another step in the offing, and when I eventually took it, it was to have far greater consequences.

All these years I'd been going to the music publishers, shopping for new songs. The people in all the publishers' offices knew me and were kind to me, but the closest, kindest friend of the lot was Walter 'Wally' Ridley. He later became a producer for EMI Records, but in those days he worked on the 'exploitation' side of the music publishing house of Peter Maurice in Denmark Street. An exploitationist would try to match the right song with the right artiste, and Wally always kept his eyes and ears open for songs he thought might suit me, he'd keep an eye on the music they wrote or bought in from the songwriters doing the rounds and would play what he deemed the best or most appropriate over on the piano for me, and generally offered encouragement and advice – he was a talented singer and composer himself. Naturally there was a Denmark Street grapevine, and through this Wally came to know that a very promising young bandleader named Joe Loss was looking for a girl singer for some radio broadcasts he'd got coming up. Wally suggested that I should try to get an audition, and in fact persuaded Joe to come over to the office. Wally played for me and I sang for Joe. To my delight Joe, with no hesitation, said, 'Yes. Fine,' and that was it. I hadn't had time to get worked up or nervous about it, but there I was, at one jump, lined up to do my first broadcast. To the generation brought up on records and television, the chance of a live broadcast on sound only, at a time when there were still plenty of people who didn't have a radio at all, can hardly appear to be anything to get excited about. But in 1935 wireless listening was growing in popularity and to get on the radio was the biggest single opportunity that could come the way of a new artist. You first proved yourself in broadcasting, and then, if you were lucky, you made your records.

This was just the start of an extraordinary sequence of events in my life at this stage. For, in the very same week that I successfully auditioned for Joe Loss, there was a further rustling of the Denmark Street grapevine, this time to the effect that band leader Charlie Kunz was auditioning for a girl singer to do some broadcasting with his Casani Club Orchestra. Wally suggested that I should try for that as well, which might have seemed unnecessary, since Joe Loss had said he'd use me. But at that time Charlie Kunz was the really big name; Joe was coming up very fast, and already had the band at the Astoria, Charing Cross Road. (The Astoria was a wonderful venue, incidentally: it was built on the site of an old pickle factory in 1893 by Edward Albert Stone, who built the four other Astorias across London (in Brixton, Streatham, Finsbury Park and the Old Kent Road). It opened as a cinema in 1927 but by the 1930s it had become a popular theatre and live music venue. That was Joe Loss's stomping ground.) Charlie Kunz, on the other hand, was far more established, he was tremendously popular and he was making records. Anybody who became associated with that band stood a good chance of going really far.

People later made out that someone connected with Charlie Kunz heard me broadcasting with Joe Loss, and that I was snapped up for the Casani Club broadcasts. The truth is rather less romantic: I went down to the Casani Club at Imperial House in Regent Street and did an orthodox audition for Charlie and the owner, Santos Casani. Santos, by the way, had been an international ballroom-dancing champion, a specialist in the once wicked tango, before he started his nightclub. That famous newsreel clip of a couple dancing the Charleston on the roof of a London taxi was a stunt fixed up by Santos Casani. He'd also been a very young pilot in the First World War.

Neither Santos nor Charlie had heard me before, as I hadn't done a broadcast by then; so it wasn't by any means a walkover or a foregone conclusion. It was between me and several other girls, and I didn't think I was really sophisticated enough for them. Eventually the choice was narrowed down to me and one other girl, and after what seemed like a good deal of debate and consultation, they picked me. I could hardly believe it – within the space of a week I'd auditioned for, and been accepted by, two very important bandleaders to do the one thing that every young singer would give her eye teeth for: to sing on the radio.

If it was a matter for a small glow of pride, it was also a matter for plenty of tact, for while there was no question of Joe Loss taking me on permanently, I had given him a verbal undertaking to do three broadcasts with him. One of the conditions of working with Charlie Kunz, however, was that I shouldn't broadcast with anyone else. But Charlie was wonderful about it – as he was about everything else – and he let me keep my word to Joe. So by the time I came to be first heard over the air, in August 1935, although it was with Joe Loss's band, I was actually signed to Charlie Kunz.

If I can remember the colour of the lilac bows on the dress I wore the first time I sang on stage, and if I can remember unpacking new plimsolls at Auntie Maggie's, I ought to recall a good deal more clearly than I do the sensation of being on that historic first broadcast. But I don't, and I think the reason must be that once I got started I broadcasted very frequently, and all the recollections have gelled into one picture of microphone, red light, song sheet, instruments and studio clock. I'm not trying to suggest that I quickly became blasé, for although I always tried to regard singing simply as my job, I don't think I ever treated it casually. The thing is that even I was surprised by the amount of radio work I did within weeks of beginning. I have a cutting headed, in my own gawky block capitals in the scrapbook I kept, 'East Ham Ecko' – I told you I couldn't spell – 'Sept. 13th 1935' that states that I'd made seven broadcasts already. Even more amazing – though I really cannot recall giving it much of a thought at the time – is that in those few weeks I was given the opportunity to reach not just a national audience but an international one, as I'd also done an Empire broadcast by then – the Empire Service being the forerunner of the World Service. With the help of this medium, through the huge clumsy microphone, I had been lifted out of East Ham and East London and given the key to the world. Or so it seemed to me. In one single month, my career had made more progress than it had in the whole previous decade, and – although I didn't really know it then, perhaps – the points had been set for the way it was to continue for some years to come.

I don't know whether it was cheek, candour or lack of being able to see where my proper future lay, but I seem to have told the writer of that *Echo* article that what I really wanted to do was to go into films. It was true. I had actually worked in a film studio even before I did my first broadcast with Joe Loss. Trivia fans might like to look out for a 1935 film called *A Fire has been Arranged*, starring Bud Flanagan and Chesney Allen – the famed comedy duo – and actor Alastair Sim, and provided you don't blink at the crucial moment you might spot me in a crowd scene. It all came about because another act appearing with me at a club in Woolwich one night said they did some occasional film extra work, and why didn't I try it – it might be a way of getting my nose into something new. I was given the address of an agent and not long afterwards I went along and put my name on the books. When they asked me what I could do, I said I was a singer.

'What else? Can you ride a horse?'

'Yes.' (I couldn't.)

'Can you play tennis?'

'Yes.' (I was a lousy, if keen, tennis player.)

I said yes to everything, because I was convinced they'd never send for me. And of course they did, and I had to go to Twickenham, not, as it happened, to ride horses and play tennis and sing, but to wander about those terrible front sets at the very generous rate of one pound a day. For this infinitesimal part I made myself a whole outfit in grey flannel, including a big cape with a red lining, and a little grey hat. When the film came to the local cinema I just had to go and see it, and Mum came with me. I caught a glimpse of myself wandering by in a street scene, and that was it – my first and only piece of film extra work, but it had been enough, obviously, to whet my appetite. That I got the chance later to star in three films had nothing to do with that little episode, but arose out of my real career as a singer.

This crowd work led, indirectly, to another strange little episode. At the top end of Charing Cross Road there was an Express Dairy Tea Room, where I used to go after I'd been the rounds of the publishers' offices. It was used a lot by theatrical and musical pros, and I was sitting over a cup of coffee there one day when a tall, thin young man struck up a conversation with me. It emerged that he was out of work, and on the strength of my recent experience in the Flanagan and Allen film, I told him he ought to try the agencies to see if there was anything going as a film extra. He thanked me and said he would. It turned out years later that I'd been talking to Cardew Robinson, the comedian and actor who became famous as 'Cardew the Cad'. (Many years later he was in *Carry On Up the Khyber* and *Last of the Summer Wine*.)

I appeared briefly in one other film during this time. It was in the great days of the 'short', a film of anything between five and fifteen minutes, which formed part of that buffer between the second feature and the big picture. The newsreel, the Disney cartoon, the travel film, the interval with the ice-creams and, in big cinemas, the organist who rose out of the floor – some, or all of these, would give the audience a chance to go to the loo and find their seats again before Clark Gable or Errol Flynn captivated them for the next hour and a half. One of a series of six 'British Lion Varieties' – the type of short that went into that slot – was by the Joe Loss band, and I sang one of the numbers, 'Love is Like a Cigarette'. I was hardly a film star, but it was an improvement on a fleeting glimpse of me in a crowd scene.

For a time I was destined to be heard rather than seen. Although I did all the Casani Club radio work with Charlie Kunz, I was never one of the regular artists at the club itself. From my point of view this was a very good arrangement, because it meant that I got the cream of the work without having to cope with those gruelling club hours, which force entertainers to become nocturnal animals and live their lives upside down, so to speak. I would do Saturday-night broadcasts with Charlie, and all his overseas programmes. Not only that: being the kind and considerate man that he was, he also used to take me on his Sunday concerts – not because he needed anyone to help him with his act, for he was enormously popular, but just to give me an extra few quid and a little more exposure and experience.

In my dress and mannerisms I must have been completely unsophisticated still, but musically he respected me, and from the start he gave me complete freedom of choice over what I sang. By that I mean he never pressed songs on me or insisted that I sang any particular number, which really was a lot of rope to give a girl of eighteen. Obviously he had to approve my choices, but that was the only control he imposed. I would go round the Denmark Street publishers, as I had been doing for years, and make my own selection from what was offered me. Then, no matter what publisher it had come from, Wally Ridley, in his helpful encouraging way, would find the key for me and rehearse me in it. Since, as I said before, for radio work and even for some work in front of live audiences, it was the done thing to have the song sheet in front of you, I had none of the old nightmare of learning new songs, and could concentrate on presenting them properly. It also meant that we didn't have to prepare too far ahead, and very often one week's find would be in the following week's broadcast. Once Charlie had approved my choice, it would be given to one of his music arrangers, usually Art Strauss, and that would be it. If you could assure the publishers in advance that you would be able to sing the song over the air not fewer than three times, they would often undertake to pay for the arrangement themselves.

That was perfectly fair and above board. But this was also the golden age of 'plug money', the undisguised backhander from a publisher's plugger to a bandleader or a singer in exchange for an undertaking to perform a given song over the air. Some bandleaders made a lot of money in this way, and some vocalists, too, did quite well out of it. But apart from the ethics of the thing, it always struck me as a very dangerous game to play. The risk of being stuck with an unsuitable number appeared to me to far outweigh the short-term benefit of a tax-free fiver. A singer should be grateful for the occasional *right* song when it comes along, for it'll do her more good than any amount of under-the-counter subsidy. I was the target of this sort of approach, of course, because as soon as anyone started broadcasting they'd be sent stacks of music, and one or two people left you in no doubt that there'd be a little something for you in an envelope if you just happened to choose the piece they were working on. But it quickly became obvious that I had very clear ideas of what lay within my emotional and technical range, and wouldn't be diverted from them, and after that I was left alone.

It was at this period – on the edge of big things, as it were – that I realized that the entertainment business could bring conflicting emotions. One day, going up to the West End on the bus on the way to do a broadcast, with my cloth coat over my long dress and my song copies rolled up under my arm, I'd be assailed by two contradictory feelings at once. I'd be so nervous that I would find myself wishing that something – anything – would happen to the bus to hold it up so that I wouldn't have to go. Why have I let myself in for all this? I'd ask myself as we rattled down the East India Dock Road. At the same time I used to get a little smug glow out of looking at the other passengers and thinking, Wouldn't all you lot be surprised to know that this young lady sitting so quietly in the middle of you was on her way to do a broadcast?

Within a few weeks of starting to broadcast with Charlie Kunz I was also making records with the Casani Club Band. The first one was 'I'm in the Mood for Love', a very pretty Jimmy McHugh–Dorothy Fields song from a 1935 film called *Every Night at Eight*. It's extremely satisfying to know that not only was it popular at that time, but it went on being popular and became a standard. It wasn't a hit for me particularly, but at least it meant I could rely on my nose for a good song. That wasn't my first record, though. Right at the start of 1935 I'd gone into a private studio with Howard Baker's band and recorded a song called 'Home'. It was on the label of Teledisk, a firm which specialized in making records for individuals – a bandleader might have one of his own broadcasts recorded, for example – and it was never issued commercially. In the spring of 1935 I also began to record anonymously for the Crown label; they made those eight-inch records that were sold in Woolworth's. Strangely enough I sold over a million records on the Crown label long before I was known as the Forces' sweetheart. They also produced all sorts of people no one will remember now: Al Jolson, Al Bowlly, Mrs Jack Hylton and the unlikely star Sir Henry Cooper (who sang 'I'm Enery the Eighth, I Am'). They would have a popular song on one side of the record and a song nobody knew on the other.

I feel sad in a way that I never walked into a branch of Woolworth's and saw one of my records – or at least I don't remember ever doing that. Years later in 2008 when Woolworth's shut down, nostalgic news reports made much of the fact that I made my first record with them. I knew people bought the records – otherwise they wouldn't have kept on making them – but I never saw a copy of one of my records in someone else's house. I was on ever so many Crown records after that, though sometimes with Rossini's Accordion Band and all sorts of strange little groups. The name of the firm that actually made them was Chrystallate, and their musical director was a well-known bandleader from what you might call the second division of British dance orchestras of the day, Jay Wilbur. Chrystallate had studios in Broadhurst Gardens, West Hampstead, which became the Decca studios when Decca took over the firm in 1938. Crown's policy was to put a popular song – a published copyright song – on one side of the record, and a song nobody knew, an unpublished number which they bought outright from the composer, on the other. They snapped up hundreds of such songs at ten pounds a batch and they'd go through them every so often to see what would suit any given artist.

For Crown, although at first I appeared completely anonymously, as time went on and my name began to have a little value I was billed on the label, in small letters: 'With Vocal Refrain by Vera Lynn'. I didn't get any more money for that, but it was assumed that it helped the record a little. I never, incidentally, recorded under another name. It was Vera Lynn or nothing.

My first solo record was on Crown, too, and it's obvious from this that, although I couldn't broadcast with anybody but Charlie Kunz, I was allowed to make records under my own name. 'Up the Wooden Hill to Bedfordshire' was the A side (though I don't remember anyone using that term then) and it was backed with 'That's What Loneliness Means to Me'. I can remember the first line: 'A grain of sand in the desert …' I was accompanied by Charles Smart at the organ, and it was released in February 1936. By then the enormous power of radio had done a great deal for me. The Crown release sheet said I was 'Already famous as a vocalist with Charlie Kunz' and publishers were finding my name worth putting on their advertisements. Two of the songs I performed over the radio right at the beginning were 'If My Love Could Talk' and 'Ev'ry Day'. The firm that published them started using my picture in their advertising more or less straight away and I began to get a gratifyingly large amount of fan mail, which was to persist for the next seventy years – much to my surprise and delight.

By October 1935, I'd graduated from the *East Ham Echo* (which I'd at last learned to spell) to getting my picture in the *Daily Sketch*. I'm left with the horrible feeling that there was only one picture of me at the time – parting on the right, hair tumbling to just north of my shoulders, one of which, the left, is hunched slightly forward so that I'm looking over it at the camera. Doubtless I was under photographer's orders. In this engaging pose I appear to have gazed out at all the newspaper readers in Britain during the first week in November 1935.

This was my first taste of stardom. You didn't worry about image, you just were whoever you were and you made the best of yourself. There wasn't this idea that you had to get into the papers. You just did your job and if the press wanted an article, they did it. You had your own photographs done for fan mail, because people used to write in for them, but there were none of these photo shoots you have nowadays. Later, when I used to perform in the theatres during the war, you would get reporters dropping by and wanting an interview. I hear that you don't get that now: reporters wouldn't think it worthwhile going round the theatres and asking for interviews. Today you would organize it, and I understand they pay money for these interviews. In those days you were only too pleased to get the publicity and nobody paid for anything. What was nice was that you could be quite famous but also anonymous. I did four years of solid broadcasting on the radio at a time before television, so by the time the war came along, I was well known. But people didn't recognize me in the street: they knew my voice and what I sounded like, but not necessarily what I looked like; I could still take the bus.

Oddly, I've no recollection of how it felt to have made this sudden step up. What stays much more clearly in my memory is the gentle shyness of Charlie Kunz. It's become such a cliché to say this or that entertainer is really a shy person underneath that people tend to smile cynically when they hear it, but Charlie Kunz, for all his great popularity, was a genuinely shy man. He'd come to fame with a piano style that was as gentle as he was, very easy on the ear and simple enough to make his listeners feel that with a spot of practice they could do it too. (Bing Crosby sang like that; every bathroom in the country had a Bing Crosby in it.) The Casani Club was always well patronized, Charlie's broadcasts attracted huge audiences and his records sold well. By the standards of show business he was entitled to a swollen head, but he wasn't the sort.

The Casani Club was in Regent Street, just before you came to the curve – the old Quadrant – and I was in the crowd in the street outside it one New Year's Eve with Charlie and his wife, who was as delightful a person as he was. The club was on the first floor, and a large section of this noisy, good-humoured throng was looking up at the windows and chanting, 'We want Charlie; we want Charlie …' over and over again. If they'd known he was actually down there among them they'd have mobbed him. So he stood huddled between us while we all three adopted the best camouflage we could by joining in the shouting. It was wonderful to see this retiring little man shouting out his own name in self-protection. And because everyone was shouting for him, I felt extremely proud to be with him.

My family, meanwhile, were beginning to enjoy my success. All the money I had earned had gone into the house up to this point. My mother had been very good at managing the finances: she had her own customers for her dressmaking business and she was the secretary of the women's section at the local working men's club, so she was good with figures. Until I was in my late teens she took the money and put it into the housekeeping. I have no idea what happened to it.

It was around this time – as I approached twenty – that I started managing my own affairs. I didn't think much about this kind of thing, but I did eventually get myself an account with Lloyds. I think it must have been fairly unusual for a young woman of my age to have her own bank account in the late 1930s.

I spent a very happy eighteen months with Charlie, singing on his broadcasts and at his concerts, appearing on his records – again 'With Vocal Refrain by Vera Lynn' – and enjoying the company of him and his wife. At every stage of my career I've always been surprised and delighted to have got as far as I did at any given moment, and being with Charlie Kunz was far more than I'd have hoped for two years earlier. At the same time I also understood that as long as people accept you there are certain logical steps you can expect to follow. By 1937, I suppose I must have been ready for the next one: a step up into the biggest band in the land.

CHAPTER FOUR

A Taste of Ambrosia

B ert Ambrose must have been the most reluctant boss I've ever had.

Billy Cotton, who later was good enough to regret it, had sent me home after a week and a half with his band; Henry Hall, who had auditioned me sometime between the Billy Cotton episode and the broadcasts with Joe Loss and Charlie Kunz, didn't want to know. I may have been disappointed at the time, but at least they made up their minds in the light of what they considered was right for their music. Ambrose practically had to have his arm twisted before he'd take me on, and even then for a long time he didn't seem to be sure if he'd done the right thing. In the end I stayed with him for three and a half years and he made about as much fuss over letting me go as he had about letting me join. As we shall see, bandleaders used to be a strange breed where their singers were concerned.

The arm-twisting was done in early 1937 by Joe Brannelly, an American musician who'd been associated with Ambrose since the late twenties, first as a guitarist and later as personal manager. I was almost twenty years old. Brannelly was very friendly with the crowd from the Peter Maurice publishing house, as I was, and looking back on it now I feel it was a case of any friend of theirs was a friend of mine. He was always in there, talking shop with Wally. I was always in there too. Joe had watched my progress and now he thought I was ready to sing with the Ambrose band. (As for Wally, he went on to work with Alma Cogan in the 1950s and was responsible for releasing Elvis's 'Heartbreak Hotel' in the UK. That man loved the popular song business more than just about any other person I know, right up until his death in February 2007.)

There were other dance bands that broadcast a great deal, and others that worked the best-paid society jobs, such as Jack Harris's, but no other leader had such a reputation in both fields as Ambrose. He managed to be both popular and exclusive at the same time, and had what was generally agreed to be the best band in Britain. To sing with him implied that the vocalist had risen to somewhere near the top of the tree. As Ambrose was under no illusion about that, he obviously wasn't going to bestow this automatic recognition lightly, and while he must have trusted Joe Brannelly's judgement to an extent, he certainly didn't believe I was right for the band.

To start with, he had one female vocalist already, Evelyn Dall, an American girl, very glamorous, blonde and sophisticated in her manner and dress, if not in her songs; she did all the bright, breezy numbers and was a bit of a comedienne in her own way. For most of the ballads he had a great singer in Sam Browne, so he could well have felt he didn't need another voice. Secondly, he did after all have the number-one Mayfair society band, and I was still a very gauche, unpolished young woman. Girls mature more quickly these days, but even for the time I was a slow developer, so that at just twenty I still had very little dress sense, no chic (whatever happened to that word?) and no real idea of how to make the most of myself. With my unashamed cockney background I'm sure he thought I was a little too much from the wrong side of the street for a band like his. I could almost see his point. He had been leader of the band at the Embassy Club and the Café de Paris in the thirties, and I later discovered that his salary as musical director at the Mayfair Hotel, right back in 1927, had been £10,000 a year. He'd been successful in America before that too. I, on the other hand, had still fresh in my memory the time when, at about fourteen, I was the Fairy Queen in some third-rate pantomime and I overheard another member of the cast saying – of me – 'She'll never get anywhere: she's too common.'

Joe Brannelly persisted, however, and finally persuaded Ambrose that, if he wouldn't give me a chance on his BBC broadcasts, then he ought to put me into some of the Radio Luxembourg programmes he was doing for a show called *Up To The Minute Rhythm Music* sponsored by Lifebuoy Toilet Soap. That's how I happened to make my debut with Ambrose in the Luxembourg studios at Bush House, by courtesy of a brand of soap. (Sometime after that I also did a series for Sanpic disinfectant. Hygiene by radio was all the rage in the thirties.) As a matter of fact there was much more commercial radio around in this country than some people realize. There was not only Luxembourg but Normandy, Poste Parisien and Lyons as well.

Ambrose, still unconvinced, I think, used me very sparingly, letting me do only one or at the most two songs per programme, but it was enough to start the fan mail coming in. Finally, Joe talked him into trying me out on some BBC broadcasts – again strictly rationed to one song to a show – and I suppose he got enough letters to prove a point and he finally kept me on. To tell the truth, it was a little embarrassing really, because apparently my solitary number often drew a bigger postbag than anything else in the programme. It was a strange situation. He was clearly more attracted to the kind of person and performer that Evelyn Dall represented, and probably couldn't see exactly where my appeal lay. But he liked my singing, if only because the musician in him could appreciate how in tune I was. I shall never forget a time up in that big old studio on the eighth floor of Broadcasting House, when I'd just sung 'O Sole Mio' on an important radio show. 'Boy, that was great – every note so clear,' he said to me. Such a compliment! I thought then that either he'd got used to me or perhaps he'd actually come round to liking me.

Ambrose – or Ammy, as we called him – treated me very well, and so did the boys in the band. Evelyn was the only one who gave me a hard time, and I'm sorry to say she seemed to resent my being there right from the start. I hated arguments and rows, and still do, and I would do almost anything to avoid quarrelling with somebody. I realize now that I was too easy going, and instead of letting her sit on me the way she did I should have blown my top. The more I tried to be friendly with her the more she would freeze me out. Most of the fellows in the band, who were always wonderful to me, were a little on their guard with her too, largely on account of the relationship that was presumed to exist between her and Ammy. Certainly she got top billing and the number-one dressing room even long after Ambrose himself had started to admit that I was doing more than my share of pulling the audience. But although the way she treated me eventually came to a head, tolerating it was worth it to be with such a great band, and I had a good time on the whole. Besides, I was fulfilling the only ambition I ever had: to be the best singer in the biggest band in the land.

The routine for finding my songs was much the same as it had been when I was with Charlie Kunz. No matter who you were, you haunted the music publishers' premises, but the better known you were, the greater the chance of being invited into the manager's office – where there was both a piano *and* a carpet – to be shown the choicest items in stock. If you indicated an interest in anything, a pianist would be brought out of his room down the corridor. 'Play Miss Lynn this song,' he'd be told. It was all very different from the beginning of your career, when you were lucky to get into any of the rooms and you were only too glad to find anybody at all to play the songs over at the piano for you.

When I was with Ambrose the days of the composer/ performer were still a long way off, and the Denmark Street offices were literally the market place where professional songwriters put their goods on show. If you were looking for something to record on your own account – that is, under your own name, and not simply as the vocalist with a band – and you came across a song you fancied, the first thing you'd ask was: 'Who else has seen this?' We all regarded it as essential not to make a record of a number that some other singer had just done. Actually, the popular record business existed on two levels, in a way. There were the current hits, which all bands would have in their repertoire merely to stay up to date, and of which several bands would record their version. Then there were items that would become identified with one particular band or performer, and it was here that an instinct for picking a song was so important, and where radio played such a huge part. People really *listened* in those days, and they put down their reactions on paper; it was tremendously satisfying, after you'd found a song that you thought was good, to get fan mail from listeners telling you they thought so too. Then the song would be programmed until another instinct told you that it was worn out. It stands to reason that the insinuating phrase 'The plug money's on if you could do this song' wasn't going to be used in connection with something that you'd decided to sing already. Conversely, if they were willing to slip you a fiver for doing it, the chances were that it was not your type of song anyway. 'Yours' and 'We'll Meet Again', which would both be found on publishers' shelves in the not-too-distant future, needed no plug money to get them moving.

All this song-shopping set-up – the cubicles with their own pianists, the stock of reach-me-down songs waiting for customers to come and try them, the aspiring composers and lyric writers hawking their manuscripts – was swept aside when the beat groups became big, using stuff they'd written themselves, or that had been written for them, or which they'd picked up from earlier rhythm and blues records. It happened in America first. I can remember visitors from transatlantic music publishers saying, 'In America that's all gone now; there are music publishers' offices in New York where you won't even find a piano.' We thought it couldn't happen here, but it did, of course.

But back then I chose my own songs when I was with Bert Ambrose just as I had with Charlie Kunz, and in another respect the job was similar – to start with I wasn't a full-time member of the band, merely joining him for radio work and records. As I said, Bert didn't exactly over-use me on broadcasts, not helped by the fact that in 1937, at just about the time I started to work with Ambrose, the BBC went through one of its periodic bouts of wishing to do the public good, and decreed that not more than one number in three in a broadcast by a dance band could be a vocal. I'm sure that it meant well, and hoped to protect our morals from laxity and our language from Americanization, but in view of the fact that almost all the new numbers were vocals, and that instrumentals were starting to become rarities, it was a completely unrealistic idea. The mere fact that a dance band couldn't exist without its singers – sorry, crooners – was a clear pointer to the way things really were. The BBC had always been a bit patronizing towards dance music and had tried to keep a schoolmasterly eye on it even in the twenties, and for years to come it would try to shield the public from what it came to call 'slush' – which sometimes meant me.

This rationing of vocals to one in every three numbers was part of the same BBC thinking that thirty years later would give Johnny Speight an allocation of so many swear words to a page of script for Alf Garnett to use in the *Till Death Us Do Part* series on television. If you sit down and work it out, you can see the fatherly concern that lay behind it all; unfortunately, it merely succeeded in making the BBC look silly. The profession was so incensed about it that singers formed themselves into the Radio Crooners' Association. Since one of the things we were supposed to be objecting to was the name 'crooner' itself, it doesn't seem a very appropriate title, and not a lot was heard of the association, but at least it showed how high our feelings ran at the time.

The period 1937–38 was a strange one for the dance band world anyway. Many bandleaders all of a sudden found themselves having a tough time economically, and there was a good deal of hoo-ha about musicians being asked to take cuts in their salary. With the rather uncertain state of the record industry at the time, I remember that during 1937 Ambrose stopped recording because of a dispute with Decca, who wanted to renew his contract at a lower fee. Their case was that the business was in a state of depression and was going to have to economize or go under, so it was that in the winter of 1937–38, presumably for reasons tied up with all these events, Bert Ambrose temporarily broke up the big band and formed first a sextet plus vocalists and then the Ambrose Octet, which toured the variety theatres at the top of the bill.

It was then that I joined him full time, and the first reviews I have among my old cuttings seem to suggest that one of the sextet's earliest important appearances was in January 1938, at the Holborn Empire. It was a good little show, consisting of what one reviewer rightly called 'the cream of Ambrose's

Right: Aged 1.

Left: In sequins and tulle netting for an early performance – one of my mother's creations.

Right: A lovely family shot of Mum, Dad, Roger and I.

Left: In Grandma's garden at Ladysmith Road.

Above: Another family group, with (top row) Nellie, me, George, Kath, (bottom row) Roger, Mum, Auntie Maggie, Dad, and Joan at the front.

Left: Mum and Dad on the beach.

Above: An early press shot, aged 15.

Above: Afternoon tea with Mum!

Above: Our wedding day – Harry, me and Roger.

Above: Rehearsing for 'Sincerely Yours' in 1941 with Howard Thomas and Fred Hartley.

Above: In a recording studio, singing with an orchestra.

Left: At my typewriter, answering letters.

Above: Serving tea to the troops at a YMCA tea cart.

Above: In uniform in a still from *We'll Meet Again*, 1943.

band'. We had the American-born clarinettist Danny Polo; the trumpet player was Tommy McQuater, he was very Scots and immensely kind – if I had any sort of argument or dispute with Ammy, he would help fight my battles, and he did what he could to lessen the bad atmosphere between Evelyn and me. Tommy was also the most helpful member of the group when it came to giving me a hand with the large trunk I always had my dresses and shoes in. We had two members, who apart from being great musicians were also good comedians in their own right: Les Carew, the trombonist, and our larger-than-life drummer, Max Bacon. Max Bacon's line was to tell hopelessly garbled versions of nursery rhymes and fairy tales using a unique variety of East End–Jewish dialect which would now be seen as hopelessly politically incorrect. On piano we had Bobby McGee, and the bass player was Tiny Winters, who used to do the occasional vocal when he had been with Lew Stone's band earlier in the thirties, and startled everybody who heard him for the first time by having an incredibly high voice. The singers in that early stage act were Evelyn Dall, the Three Admirals and me, and the package as a whole headed a bill that included a trick cycling act, Naunton Wayne (who was a seasoned cabaret performer and compere before finding fame in Hitchcock's *The Lady Vanishes*) and a puppet that did the Big Apple – the dancing craze of the year. For me it was like a homecoming, a glamorous return to solo stage work, and I thoroughly enjoyed myself.

I was having a minor success at the time with a record of a song which was then more than twenty years old, 'The Bells of St Mary's' by Douglas Furber (who wrote 'Limehouse Blues') and A. Emmett Adams, and of course I sang it in the show. One night I nearly didn't. I was just waiting to go on when I realized I couldn't remember the words. This was typical of the nerves that dogged me throughout my career and was one of the only episodes where, to my horror, I actually found myself giving into them. I suppose I must have gone on – but from then on I never appeared on stage without having a copy of a new song to glance at just before I went on.

In the years since the Ambrose period of my life, I have learned from people who were around at the time and closer to him than I was a little more about his motives for employing me, as it were, almost against his will. He always liked to feel that he had around him the best people he could get, and even if I didn't buy my clothes from the right places or use the right perfumes or go to the 'in' hairdresser, I had a clearly marked style of my own and that's what counted with him. That much, as I say, I found out later. But I got an inkling of my value to him while I was still with him. I had decided I couldn't take the atmosphere that Evelyn Dall's hostility to me was creating any longer, and had told Ammy that I was going to leave. Evelyn was younger than me and she had always been very unfriendly towards me. Although she didn't speak to me – she ignored me – I used to keep trying to befriend her and talk to her, but as far as she was concerned, I didn't exist. Eventually I wanted to walk out – and it was no idle threat, I genuinely felt that it would be the best thing all round if I left. I realized that I'd be giving up an immense amount of prestige, because there really wasn't anything higher than the Ambrose level in the kind of work I was doing, but I gave him

my notice. It must have been during one of the Octet inter-
ludes, for it was not Ammy's practice actually to travel round
with the smaller unit, and I know that on the occasion I'm
thinking about he had to make a long journey – up north or
maybe even to Glasgow or somewhere like that – especially to
see me. He came all the way from London with an offer to
double my salary if I would stay on.

I could hardly refuse, but even without the money I probably would have agreed. I'd have been flattered enough that the
leader of our finest band had travelled a long way just to ask
me to remain with him. After all, I didn't *want* to leave, and
Ammy's concern was all I needed to convince me that it was
unnecessary.

To go from a weekly pay packet of £20 to £40 in one
jump was, to me, at the age of twenty-one or so, tangible
evidence of progress. It was also, in absolute terms, a lot of
money. When my grandmother had moved into Ladysmith
Avenue before the 1920s, the rent was nine-and-sixpence a
week for the whole house (she could have bought it for £150,
but didn't, for even that was well beyond her reach), and
although prices were on the increase, I don't think they'd gone
up that much by the late thirties. Although we'd never gone
without, during the Depression my father had sometimes been
out of work and we'd seen the economic sense of those broken
biscuits and two penn'orth of yesterday's cakes (a cake more
than twenty-four hours old was very rightly held to be stale
when I was a child, and you could get a whole bagful for
tuppence). We certainly didn't have any money to chuck
about, so the value of it was never lost on me. But I don't

believe I ever consciously thought of wealth when I started to earn money by singing. It was some little time before I was even old enough to relate the two – performing and money – and to understand that it was possible to advance. And when I did, my fantasies were never too wild. The most I wanted was a nice house. Even when I was young, walking to school in the morning I'd take notice of the features of houses that I liked and put them together in a sort of identikit dream house. I was always doing drawings of the place I wanted, but it was never a mansion in the country or anything impractical like that. I've always been afraid to expect too much, so it was always a fairly modest establishment. Even after I'd been broadcasting regularly with Charlie Kunz and making records, I would never allow myself to believe I was better off than I was. I was lucky to have a good job, which I enjoyed, and that was as far as I'd go.

It was only slowly that the telephone's constant ringing in the parlour, the association with Charlie Kunz and Bert Ambrose, and the appearance of my name in the *Radio Times* and on posters all combined to make me understand that I was beginning to lead a different life. My mother handled my finances with great care and prudence, so there was no danger of my squandering money even if I had fancied the idea. But I did one thing that every young girl wanted to do in the thirties, and bought myself a fur coat. I paid £75 for it, which horrified my mother and rather astonishes me now when I think about it. But at least it lasted. It is hanging in my daughter Virginia's cupboard to this day in the form of a short jacket.

I was also able to do what few people could do at that time, and got myself a car. I'd always seen the sense in having a car while I was still working the clubs, and I made up my mind that as soon as I was earning £10 a week I'd buy one. When the time came, it was actually a toss-up between that and a houseboat at Westcliff. We used to go down to Southend when we were young and stand by the water watching the houseboats. I always thought how nice it would be to have a houseboat and go down and spend time there. As usual over such a grave matter there was a family discussion, and common sense settled it in favour of the car. The houseboat would be all very pleasant, but, if I were a success in my work, when would I get a chance to enjoy it? And if I wasn't, then I wouldn't be able to afford to keep it up anyway. Whereas a car would at least help me for as long as I was working.

So that's how I came to acquire a green Austin 10, cabriolet top, registration number HV 8777, at a cost of £200. I paid extra because I wanted a canvas top. One of the first journeys I made in it was to Weybourne, partly because I wanted to show off, and partly because I couldn't wait to be back there. I learnt to drive at a local driving school at a time when very few women learned to drive – and even fewer owned their own cars. I kept that car for ten years, and when I finally sold it, I got £100 more than I gave for it! I'm surprised it lasted that long, really, for at the beginning I was always forgetting that it didn't just run on nothing, and that it needed petrol and oil and water occasionally. I was always being lectured by the garage men, whose patience I must have sorely tried for the first couple of years. I wasn't at all worried, though, and I passed my driving test first time. Mind you, there wasn't the traffic that you get on the road nowadays and 30 mph was the most you could do.

So now I had a fur coat and a little green car but back home there was no proper bathroom – or indoor toilet. That was the next thing I felt I was entitled to, as I began to see the irony of getting myself up for a show or an important broadcast yet having to make do with a bath in the kitchen. (It was one of those that had a sort of lid to it which formed a table top or working surface when it was closed.) In a purely practical sense I needed something better and by now I could afford it. What am I working for? I wondered to myself. Here I am, just getting into my twenties, with a wonderful job and earning good money, still living in my grandmother's little terrace house with an outside toilet and baths by arrangement with the rest of the family. Clearly, we, or I, had to move. This was the only time I ever acted in a way that could have disrupted the family, and I told my mother that either we'd all got to move out of Grandma's house or I would take a flat in town on my own. My mother could see that I meant it, and agreed to the idea of finding another house. The next question was: did Grandma want to come with us? Except for the early years of her marriage in Thackeray Road, Mum had always lived with my grandmother and she didn't want to leave her now. But the old lady, predictably, decided to stay where she was and I set about house-hunting on my own behalf for the first time in my life.

You'll have a job believing that the nine-room house we found, solidly built during the late twenties in a quiet road in Barking, was up for sale at £1,175. In 1938 the buyer still had some say, and we even got something taken off the price. (The full Ambrose band was in temporary existence at the time, and during the actual negotiations I was away in Dublin as part of an hour-long band show.) Thus I became the owner of what estate agents call 'a desirable residence', and the little we'd saved on the price paid for it to be redecorated from top to bottom. Better than anything else, though, I could have a bath when I liked. I suppose it was quite something for a young woman to buy a house – I was certainly the only one amongst my friends to do so. But I never thought of it as particularly unusual: I was just working, earning money, and I wanted to do the best with it.

If the house was a thrill on a personal level, working with Ambrose was still providing fresh professional excitements. One of them was television. Television in this country made such a slow start when it came back after the war, in 1946, that it is easy to forget that the first public television service in the world began here ten years earlier. It's true that reception was confined to a quite limited area in the south-east of England, and to a rather small number of well-off families (the first cookery programmes were billed in the *Radio Times* as 'Cook's Night Off'), but there were some fairly lavish productions. Many of the early acts were dancers and jugglers and other visual turns which couldn't make the transition from the stage to radio, but the radio stars were also in there very early on. The dance bands were a natural choice, since most of them had to be able to mount a stage show as part of their liveli-hood. As a member of the Ambrose band, therefore, in 1938 I found myself at Alexandra Palace, wearing an atrocious, rather dark, almost mauveish make-up, applied so thickly it practically caused round shoulders. I think fabric colours were a problem, too, and I seem to remember that for a dress to appear white on the screen it actually had to be a fairly strong yellow. There was no recording, of course, so everything was done live, and when a band appeared it would usually be on twice in the same week, usually for a half-hour show. Thursday and Saturday was a common combination, I recall, and we would do different numbers, not repeats of the previous ones. It was very interesting, and with the primitive cameras of those days we were much more restricted in movement: you had to stick to your chalk mark on the floor like glue.

One night after appearing on television, I'd got Max Bacon, who was heavy enough for two ordinary people, and a couple of other members of the band in my car. It was pouring with rain and we were coming down the steep slope that leads away from Alexandra Palace. 'You're going too fast, Vera,' one of the boys said. With the prompt reactions of a veteran driver of nearly a whole year's experience, I decided that the infallible cure for going too fast was to put my foot on the brake. The skid that followed must have been really spectacular. From inside the car we appeared to lurch first one way and then the other, each time leaning over a little more. I was in no state to count the lurches, but soon enough the car turned right over on its side. We had to clamber out through a window, and I promptly had a fit of the giggles. Some woman had seen the whole thing from her bedroom window and came running out to help, but the boys said: 'The best thing for you, Vera, is to get straight back in and start driving' –

which I tried to do as soon as they'd managed to right it. But if we, by some miracle, weren't damaged, the car was. The garage man, who once again had to rescue it, diagnosed a broken back axle and gave me another, sterner lecture. My mother was in a constant state of anxiety during the first couple of years of my car-driving life, and on reflection I think she had every right to be.

All that, however, was incidental to the job. The music was the main thing, and my constant joy. And let me emphasize once again what a marvellous band Ammy had. In the purely technical sense he wasn't a great musician; he was a just-about-competent violinist and, like most bandleaders, he didn't really conduct in the true meaning of the word. But he knew exactly what he wanted and, more important for some-one who has to make not only his own living but that of perhaps twenty other people as well, he knew what his public wanted. He had a shrewd idea of how to achieve the sound he was after, and he paid good money to get the best people. He was very exacting, and if he didn't like what he heard at a rehearsal he had one famous gesture: he'd bob his head forward slightly, throw his arms back over his shoulders and make a noise which sounded like: 'Ueeergh!' Sometimes he'd add: 'You're sounding like a piece of string!'

He was moody, too. If he didn't like the way they were playing, or if he thought they were playing too loudly, he'd send half the musicians home in the middle of a gig. It wasn't unknown for him to put in a personal appearance, start playing his fiddle, stroll over to Ernie Lewis, who was leading the band towards the latter end of my stay with it, and say out of the side of his mouth: 'Tell the brass section to go home.' And if anyone forgot themselves so far as to cut loose on a somewhat jazzy chorus at a point where Ammy didn't think it was called for, he'd go to Ernie Lewis and say loudly: 'What's he doing?'

The moods extended to the way he treated the public sometimes. The full band did a tour of Holland in 1938, which was a tremendous success except, for some reason, in Utrecht. This was the first time I had travelled abroad. We rolled up at the place where we were to play, and we started to pile out of the coach while Ammy went to look at the hall and see how the bookings were going. Apparently the state of the box office dissatisfied him. 'I'm not going to do a show here,' he said. 'Come on, all out, everybody back on the coach.' So we all trooped back into the bus and drove off again. I was thunderstruck. I thought surely the show had to go on, no matter how few people there were; I'd always been brought up to believe that you had to go on and give a performance. It staggered me, though after a while I came to accept that he was just like that sometimes.

Perhaps the best known of Ammy's extra-musical activities was gambling. He was a compulsive, inveterate gambler, and there are plenty of stories of the band doing an extended engagement at Monte Carlo, and Ambrose losing their entire salary at the tables before the boys themselves could get their hands on it. He must have won occasionally, but he really did lose thousands at a time in gambling clubs, and it was a strain even on his enormous income (and it was enormous; at some jobs he'd get £100 extra an evening for himself just for being there in person).

Max Bacon was the band's other gambler, and it was because somebody knew about this that I got a sharp lesson in how naïve I still was in the ways of the world. One day the telephone rang at home and a man's voice said that Max Bacon was in trouble and urgently needed a couple of quid and could I bring it to him. Naturally I was happy to help Max out of whatever bother he was in, and set off for some address in Aldgate that the caller gave me. It took ages to find it, and when I eventually arrived, there was no Max, only the man who'd made the call. He gave me some explanation for Max's not being there and said, 'Have you got the money?' and I gave it to him and went home again. When I saw Max later I innocently asked him if he'd got his money all right and of course he knew nothing about it. I realized then that I'd been conned in a small but elaborate way, and started to wonder: why go to all that fuss for a couple of pounds? I've not the faintest idea who the man was, but the point is that he knew Max was a terrible gambler, and was always borrowing money, and he presumably knew also that I was a soft touch for what anybody else would have realized was a ridiculous story.

It may be that extreme innocence was a kind of shield, for I recall another incident that took place rather earlier, while I was still working for Charlie Kunz. I was leaving the Casani Club one night after a broadcast and was waiting for a bus home (my mother remained adamant that it was straight home after a show – no parties or dancing) when some man came up to the bus stop and started to talk. He asked me what I was doing and I blandly told him I was waiting for a bus. He talked for a long time, and asked me all sorts of questions, which I politely and gravely answered as well as I could. Finally the bus came up and this man, equally gravely, said: 'Thank you for letting me talk to you. It's not often I get a chance to talk to a nice girl like you.' I was about halfway home before I tumbled to it that it had been a big try-on, and that he'd been chatting me up. I really was that green – experienced in show business, but green as a human being.

My job went on as usual. Ambrose would sporadically reform the full band for specific engagements or a month or two of touring, and then return to the octet format, and through it all I kept working. I enjoyed the friendly, professional atmosphere in the band: the boys all treated me like their little sister. I remember there was one chap who always used to look after my luggage for me whenever we toured. We always took our job seriously, but you know what musicians are like: we were always making little jokes and having a laugh. We had several male singers – one of the best of them was Denny Dennis, who later went to America – and various changes of personnel among the musicians, but the key men, like Les Carew and Max Bacon, were there pretty constantly. Sid Collins came in, ostensibly on guitar, but he was actually very good in the sketches and songs; years later he found his métier as a radio scriptwriter.

When the Second World War broke out in 1939 the band had just been assembled again, and, apart from a rather nervy few weeks when club owners, promoters, impresarios and agents tried to adjust themselves to conditions which they couldn't predict (it turned out that entertainments of all kinds boomed the moment it became obvious that we weren't going to be exterminated during the first fortnight of the war), things went on surprisingly much as usual. A total blackout – no lights of any kind – was imposed for the first week or two, and once I set off from the New Cross Empire to drive home to Barking as if by Braille. I did what I certainly wouldn't do now: I stopped to give a man a lift, to find that he lived in the next road to me. It took hours to do that normally short journey because we were not allowed any light whatsoever. Soon, masked headlamps would come in, and little torches with two layers of newspaper between the bulb and the glass, and you could begin to grope your way about again.

Otherwise, as I said, the first months of the war allowed us to lead an unexpectedly normal life. For a time it was indeed a phoney war, though there would be nothing phoney about it once it started in earnest. By the time that happened, two other major events had taken place in my own life. Professionally, I had moved from the comparative shelter of the Ambrose band. Personally, I had just met the man I was going to marry.

CHAPTER FIVE

Wild About Harry

The small, dark and handsome man who came into the Ambrose band in the late summer of 1939 was to become my husband and my manager. Harry Lewis was aggressive, humorous, persistent and a very good clarinettist and tenor saxophonist. He was very good-looking, although he was a little shorter than me. He also had the most gorgeous head of hair. Years later I remember he went to the hairdresser's up in London one time and he came back more or less completely shorn. I remember gasping, 'Your hair has all gone! And you have such lovely hair.' And I said that from then on I would trim it myself. And I did.

But that was a long way in the future. In the months before the war we were rehearsing to take the stage show on the road when we first met. It wasn't until I really got to know him that I realized that he was The One.

His arrival and the outbreak of war more or less coincided, but unlike the major powers, he began his campaign straight away. Ambrose had once again put the full band together, with Harry in the sax section, and we'd been called to Ambrose's posh flat-cum-office in Hereford House, just off

Park Lane, to be told about plans for an autumn tour. The war had not actually begun, though it couldn't have been more than a matter of weeks or even days away, for the Octet was working right up until the weekend war broke out on 1 September, and the big band was on tour by the end of September. The first public performance by the new big band was to have been a broadcast on 9 September; in fact I don't think that can have actually taken place, because in the first week or two of the war, radio programmes were drastically altered, but the tour itself went ahead more or less as planned. It was a confusing time for all of us: in the run-up to the declaration of war, we all assumed we would be out of a job. But it very quickly transpired that there would be more work for us than ever.

The briefing in Ammy's office was not, as it happened, the first time I'd met Harry, though I was never actually aware of him till then. At one stage Howard Baker had kept him on a retainer of thirty shillings a week, and there were several occasions when Harry must have been in a Howard Baker band and I was singing; I think he was even among a group of Howard's boys, from whom I got the occasional lift home after a late dance. But we never really noticed each other until that afternoon in Bert's office, when he was a new member of the Ambrose orchestra.

After the meeting Harry walked out with me and said, 'Which way are you going?' And I said, 'Well, I'm going to Denmark Street.' Harry suddenly found he had to go that way, too, and said expansively: 'Let's get a cab.' As I was to discover, he was always ready to spend money on taxi fares, but I wasn't

– neither mine nor anyone else's – and I said, rather frostily, 'No *we* won't, *I'm* going on the bus.' So we climbed aboard a bus, and of course he offered to pay my fare. It was tuppence. 'I'll pay my own, thank you,' was all he got out of that; I'd learned, you see, since the night that man had tried to chat me up going home from the Casani Club. I certainly didn't know this man well enough for him to pay my fare!

It went on like that for some time, and for weeks the most I would accept from him was some chewing gum; he was always eating it, and I didn't think that implied too much in the way of surrender. But he was persistent; the hero of a wonderful old song Frank Grumit used to sing, 'There's No One for Endurance Like the Man who Sells Insurance', had nothing on Harry. Up in Coventry one time he tried to buy me a watch – three pounds ten and encrusted with marcasites like barnacles – but I wouldn't have it. I was still not accepting presents from strange men. A touring band, however, is probably one of the most enclosed, intimate societies in the world, where you can be close friends or bitter enemies but never strangers. So in time it came to be accepted, even by me, that Harry and I would be found sitting together in the coach as we travelled the country. And we travelled a great deal during the first months of the war. In addition to the usual round of theatres and ballrooms we were very soon doing troop concerts and putting on shows at factories, so we were constantly together. We used to sit together in the coach and look at the countryside and discuss the view. As you know, I always loved the country and we both used to love those talks. Looking back, those really were innocent days, then, nicer days.

Meanwhile Ammy was none too pleased. Bandleaders were nearly always strangely possessive over their singers. Tommy Dorsey never forgave Jack Lennard for leaving him, even though his replacement was Frank Sinatra; and having built Sinatra up as a featured vocalist, he adopted an unreasonably hurt attitude when Frank went out on his own. This heavy-father behaviour emerged very strongly at any sign of a romance within a band. To be fair, the grumbling and innuendo always seemed to come more from my old nemesis Evelyn Dall than from Bert, so maybe he was not as bothered as he appeared.

While I may have been sensitive to implied criticism, Harry wasn't, and he took absolutely no notice. Years later he used to chuckle about what a rebel he looked in those days: 'My hair was almost down to my collar and I had a lapel-less jacket in 1939. Ammy couldn't handle me.' While I think 'tearaway' is too strong a word – I don't believe I'd have married a tearaway – he came from an East End environment which had certainly taught him how to stick up for himself, and for other people. This came out very strongly once during the time Jack Cooper was the male singer with the band and took it into his head to accuse me of singing flat. Harry went for him like a terrier and drove him into a corner. 'She's not singing flat; *you're* singing sharp,' he said, and we heard no more about that.

If Ambrose's disapproval was largely implicit, and comparatively mild, my mother's was intense and obvious. I suppose the idea that musicians are all vagabonds must have been with us at least since the Middle Ages, when many of them were.

Anyway, my mother instinctively shared this view, and that and the fact that Harry didn't have any money were enough to put her off. Harry's being Jewish, oddly enough, wasn't the problem. There was never any religious bias whatsoever in our family; in fact I'd go as far as to say there was no conscious attitude to any religion at all. In so far as we gave it a thought, the different religions were simply various ways of doing the same thing; we'd mixed with Jewish people all our lives, and it was a point not even worth considering.

There was no opposition from any other member of the family, and Harry and my dad took to each other right away. Mind you, Harry did have a habit of letting himself look a trifle scruffy when he wasn't actually on his way to work. He used to joke later that if a young man had shown up to call for our daughter, Virginia, looking as unshaven as he sometimes was he'd have thrown him out. But even if he had a bristly chin, he had a soft heart and a lot of determination. Very early on he announced, confidently, 'I'm going to marry you,' and I just laughed. But he kept on, and apart from anything else, I had to admire his persistence.

I'd never had a regular boyfriend, because the professional life I was leading simply didn't afford the time; nor did it leave you in one place long enough, usually, so that if any attachment were to be formed it would almost inevitably be with another member of whatever group you were touring with. Naturally the tours gave Harry opportunities, which he seized. Like the time in the train going to somewhere or other when I was sitting around watching the eternal poker game that seems to sustain musicians between gigs. The sporadic discussion turned to the subject of digs, and since I was going to somewhere I already knew, I suggested that they might like to try the place I was staying at. So Harry contrived to get himself under the same roof. These were small things, but he never missed a trick, and it was very flattering. And wherever we were we usually managed to see a few films together during the week, and even if we weren't in the same digs, Harry would walk me home.

I began to realize how serious he was one Saturday night, when I told him I was going out after the show with some young army officer, 'Oh, no you're not,' he said, getting all indignant. I pointed out to him, in my best Victorian phraseology, that we had no understanding between us, and that I could go where I liked – and I went – but when I got back (this was one of those times we were in the same digs) Harry was waiting up for me; it was very touching. All this time, of course, he was doing the usual things to impress me, like shooting a line about the fabulous car he had. When he finally turned up in it, it turned out to be a very ordinary Austin 10, and not even his but his father's. Make no mistake, though, I was getting extremely fond of him. In Liverpool once, he was kidding around and said redheads were his favourites; I took him at his word and next morning I went to the hairdresser's and came back a redhead. My mother hated that more than just about anything!

He finally proposed in deadly earnest in Brighton. We were doing a week at the Brighton Hippodrome, and a whole crowd of us decided to spend the afternoon at the pictures. At the last minute I realized I couldn't go, because Harry and I had been for a walk along Brighton beach – all bleak and empty – that morning, and I'd lost my glasses somewhere along the way. Most of my life I have had to have my glasses for driving and the cinema, and when Harry found I wasn't going with the others, he stayed behind too. And there, in this little Brighton boarding house front parlour, Harry proposed, and I accepted him. We were sitting in front of the fire and he said, 'I'm going to marry you.' Which was something he said all the time. But this time I said, 'Yes, you are.' He didn't have a ring at the time – his mother, Rachel, chose that for us later because she knew about jewellery: she chose a diamond solitaire in a platinum setting. I still wear it now, seventy years later.

That was in the winter of 1939. Very shortly after that the band was at the Glasgow Empire, and there was a restaurant opposite the stage door where we would go between and after shows. They used to have clove-coloured carnations on the tables and one night Harry sneaked one out and gave it to me. He never forgot the pleasure it gave, and every year after he gave me two dozen clove carnations on our wedding anniversary.

We would have preferred to get married within about three months of getting engaged (after all, this was wartime, and who knew what sort of future we could expect?), but that would have been too much for my mother, so we waited for another eighteen months – until 11 August 1941. The engagement had come as something of a disappointment to my parents because they were aiming a bit higher than a musician for me. I was upset about it for a while, but they soon came round when they could see that he was serious and how much he looked after me.

Becoming engaged, therefore, had only a little to do with the changes that took place in my life soon afterwards. Perhaps Harry would have thought differently about what he did if we hadn't been engaged, but what happened in March 1940, had an effect on much more than just a personal level. It had become pretty obvious that every male not entirely broken in health would sooner or later be called up, and the members of the Ambrose band faced the prospect of being picked off one by one as time went by. Nobody seems quite certain exactly who thought of it first, but it dawned on several members of the band that if they went in individually they would have no control over where they were sent, whereas if a group of them volunteered, as musicians, they stood at least a chance of remaining together as the nucleus of a working band.

Musicians are not cowards, although the press had a good time suggesting they were during the early part of the war, as leaders struggled to hang on to key personnel at least long enough to allow them to recruit competent replacements. A musician's main horror is of not being allowed to play, so, on the Monday morning of a week when we were appearing in Kilburn, eight members of the band, including George Chisholm, Tommy McQuater, Andy McDevitt and Harry, presented themselves at RAF Uxbridge, ready to fight, though preferably to play, for king and country.

I find it hard to believe that they could be so naïve, but having gone through the formalities, they turned to leave. 'Where do you think you're going?' the sergeant asked them.

They explained that they were working that night in a band. According to Harry the sergeant's reply was: 'You're not. You've had your shilling, you've got your knife, fork and spoon and you've got your towel. You're *in* all right – in the RAF.' In the end the CO had to sort it out, and they got what was technically a week's leave to finish their time with the Ambrose orchestra. All this took a while, Ammy was pacing backstage at the Kilburn Empire as the time for curtain up came nearer and there was no sign of them. 'Where have those boys got to?' he kept saying, with his arms doubled over his shoulders and a look of anguish on his face. They made it just in time, and had to go straight on, having escaped from Uxbridge by the skin of their teeth.

At the end of the week they went in for good. But they achieved what they had set out to do: they were joined by other musicians, and quickly formed a band, the Squadronnaires. Their official billing was 'The Royal Air Force No. 1 Dance Band – The Squadronnaires – appearing by permission of the Air Council'. The farther from their home base of Uxbridge the band was playing, the larger the word Squadronnaires was, and the smaller the bit about the RAF Dance Orchestra and the Air Council.

At one go, all of a sudden Ambrose had lost half his musicians, and I had acquired a fiancé in uniform. Everything was changing. At least, we told ourselves, we were all still in the entertainment business. But these were anxious times for all of us.

CHAPTER SIX

A Country at War

The mood in London changed abruptly over the next few months as people got used to being at war. The Blitz – the sustained bombing of London by the Nazi forces – was officially between 7 September 1940 and 10 May 1941, but already before then people were anxious and living in fear. It was as if we had an idea of what was to come. By May 1941 over 43,000 British civilians – half of them in London – had been killed and over a million houses were destroyed or damaged in the capital alone.

Introduced at the beginning of 1940, rationing was not as bad as it sounded. You got used to it. We ate a lot of bread and potatoes because they weren't rationed, although white bread was in very short supply (and people craved it). You could get hold of brown bread easily at first, but then there were queues for that too. Tinned goods were rationed, as were meat and cheese. Some things were impossible to get hold of, such as tea, bananas, grapes and oranges.

I tried to concentrate on my life as a singer. During the first winter of the war, Ambrose bands and Ambrose octets alternated with each other in bewildering succession. In fact, various Ambrose units must have overlapped at one period, for as 1940 opened Ammy started a new residency at the Mayfair Hotel with a twelve-piece band. Of the 600 people present at his opening night, one entertainments periodical said: 'There was a feeling of happiness and gladness that Ambrose was back among them, and that was what they gave themselves up to.' In the same month I worked with two other Ambrose groups as well: the Blue Lyres, in which I was the only vocalist, and the Octet. There was a broadcast, too, at about that time, the first for quite a while.

Apart from anything else, I suppose there hadn't been much scope for broadcasts, because a couple of days before war broke out in September 1939, the old national and regional services of the BBC had been merged into one single National Programme. (Within about twenty-four hours of the start of the war this was changed to the Home Service – a name that lived on for nearly thirty years.) The Forces Programme didn't get started until January 1940, and then just for a few hours in the evening, so for four months there was only the one network for the whole of the country, which also meant that there was less actual broadcasting being done. In February 1940, the Forces Programme expanded to a twelve-hours-a-day service, but by then, of course, for security and other reasons, direct transmission from clubs and hotels had long ceased, and the whole pattern of broadcasting had begun to change.

On top of that, the Octet had to all intents and purposes folded soon after Harry and the others joined up, for although it wasn't the Octet that went to Uxbridge, the loss of eight musicians at once from any part of his organization would have been something of a disaster for Ammy. So work of the kind I'd been doing for the past couple of years was becoming more sporadic. Everything was changing, in fact, as the spring of 1940 unfolded, and the borrowed time we'd all been living on ran out when the Germans began to show Europe what war was really like.

Even if I'd wanted to remain as a band vocalist for the rest of my life there was nowhere for me to go, because despite wartime conditions, Ambrose still had the best band there was; so the only possible step for me was to go solo. Luckily it wouldn't be a complete leap into the dark, for several reasons.

I was already making a name for myself on record in my own right. There were no charts in those days (what mattered for composers and publishers were the sales of sheet music, for pop hadn't yet become a spectator sport) and the Top Ten mentality hadn't got a grip on the industry, but record sales did occasionally get into the news. As early as January 1940, Paul Holt in the *Daily Express* wrote a piece on me, in which he says I was selling more records every month than Bing Crosby and the Mills Brothers. Well, I don't know who was doing the counting, but clearly I wasn't doing so badly. My voice, the kind of songs I liked to sing and the mood of the time were beginning to work together in my favour.

All this was even before I had come across the song that was to be associated with me for the rest of my life – 'We'll Meet Again'. In the autumn of 1939 I'd come across a number at the publishing house of Irwin Dash, written by

Ross Parker and Hughie Charles. Its lyric seemed to me to be a perfect example of what you might call the greetings card song: a very basic human message of the sort that people want to say to each other but find embarrassing actually to put into words. Ordinary English people don't, on the whole, find it easy to expose their feelings even to those closest to them. In November 1939, and for a long while after, the unpretentious off-the-peg sentiments of 'We'll Meet Again' would go at least a little way towards doing it for them. My record of it was something of a hit. Another song that became very popular was an allusion to the evacuation of children from the cities, especially London: 'Goodnight Children, Everywhere'. 'When the Lights of London Shine Again' was yet another which said what a huge number of people felt. Compared with today's sales, I doubt if the quantities were impressive, but they were good for their time and a tremendous help to me. It was some time before anyone would realize how iconic 'We'll Meet Again' would become. I feel the same about that song as when I first heard it: it's a great song and it shows how good it is that people still know it now, seventy years later. I never grew tired of singing it.

Meanwhile I was still broadcasting, even if radio work with the band had become a rarity. I did occasional radio variety shows, and in May 1940, I was given a spot in a programme built around the comedian Dicky Hassett, whose main act was based on street-market catchphrases. 'They're lovely, and they're four for three!' was one of them, though the best-known one was 'Large lumps!' It all seems faintly ridiculous now, and the idea, though a good one, wasn't enough to sustain him. The show, called *Phoney Island*, got a mixed reception, but I came out of it quite well.

As a live performer I'd already appeared during the previous two years at most of the major variety theatres in Britain as a component part of the Ambrose Octet, and there had been a number of enquiries from the variety circuits about the possibility of my doing a solo spot. The time to do something about it had definitely arrived.

While I was working for Ambrose I didn't really have an agent. Leslie McDonnell was Ammy's friend and agent, and I therefore had a kind of understanding with him. It was quite a tight little circle, actually, for the Ambrose–Leslie McDonnell friendship also included Jimmy Phillips, who was managing director of Peter Maurice, where I knew everybody and felt like one of the family. When Leslie saw that I believed it was time to move on, he said he could get me some variety dates on my own, and I told him to go ahead.

Ambrose took the customary leader's attitude – that of a mother whose daughter has threatened to leave home – and was firmly against my going solo. It meant that he was annoyed with Leslie as well, of course, because as he saw it, Leslie was encouraging me, and I suppose that it was even possible for him to believe that his own agent was working against him. Doubtless it was all smoothed over in the end, but they didn't speak to each other for a time.

It's very flattering to find that throughout July 1940 the local papers of each of the towns I appeared in took it in turn to claim that I was making my debut in variety. But, for the record, I first went on as a fully fledged solo act, with Rube Silver as my pianist, at the Coventry Hippodrome on 1 July 1940, at the age of twenty-three.

In view of the terrible pounding Coventry was to suffer in air raids the following April, it's interesting that the Saturday night BBC *Variety Programme* was broadcast live from there at the end of my first week. Security was somewhat erratic; one provincial newspaper, having dutifully said that the show would come from 'a Midland theatre', went on in the next sentence to tell its readers that 'the programme will be supported by the Coventry Hippodrome Orchestra'.

Any worries I had at that time, though, were not about security. I was simply nervy about the engagement itself, for when you realize that you are separately billed, in big letters, that you haven't got the band all round you and that you're not going to nip on and do one song and then off, you feel an enormous sense of responsibility. It was not as bad as the first time I headed a bill a year or two later in Birmingham and found my name completely across the top – that really does bring it home to you that the weight of the show is on your shoulders – but it was sobering enough. Even so, I was better off than those girls who had only ever sung with bands, for you have to go out on your own some time, and if you've never done it before it must be terribly unnerving. At least for me it was like going back to my roots, a return to where I'd started sixteen years before, with a pianist and the songs with which I'd sat on the living-room floor to learn with such difficulty. It may not have been seven-and-six for three numbers plus one-and-six for an encore any more (I believe that in that position on the bill I got £75), but the principle and, above all, the feeling were the same.

I still needed a pianist, because although there was an entire orchestra theoretically at your disposal, there was never enough time to rehearse with it properly. On a Monday band call you'd just go through the music and that was about all, so if you wanted anything tricky or even slightly elaborate, it was essential to have your own accompanist. I got Rube Silver through Harry, who'd known him as a good pianist for a long time and suggested him when it became clear that I was going out on my own. He was a very pleasant man, who did a marvellous job – he had that rare sympathy which *makes* an accompanist.

I went to places like Glasgow, Edinburgh and Wolver-hampton, enjoyed very favourable notices on the whole and steadily gained confidence in my abilities as a solo performer. Although I didn't sing with him, for a couple of weeks I was on the same bill as the man who'd turned me down a few years earlier, Henry Hall. I'm not sure how I envisaged my career progressing at that stage, but I was almost certainly prepared for a long trudge round the provincial variety theatres. As it turned out, I was in luck. I'd only been at it five or six weeks when an offer came along to go into a new production which was being prepared for the Holborn Empire. I was therefore only out in the wide world on my own for a little while before I fell into a very good show in town.

Applesauce was described in the programme as a revue, though strictly speaking I think it was more of a glorified variety show with several of the acts, like the top comedian, 'Cheeky Chappie' Max Miller and Doris Hare, who was a variety performer before becoming an actress, turning up in different spots. Afrique, then a well-known impersonator, was on the bill doing, among other things, what must have been one of the first convincing impressions of Mr Churchill, as he was then. Some papers reckoned the production was a mite too sophisticated for the Holborn Empire regulars, but most of them agreed with the writer, who thought it combined the 'attractions of spectacular revue with the more satisfying entertainment of variety'. 'You'll like the sauce,' said the *Sunday Pictorial*, 'and the apple won't give you the pip.'

Unfortunately, Londoners didn't get too much of a chance to put that to the test. The opening of *Applesauce* more or less coincided with the start of the Battle of Britain. In time, that developed into the night blitz on London, and the Holborn Empire was a fairly early casualty. It was a casualty twice over, in fact, and a good job for the cast it was. Harry was still stationed at Uxbridge and we spent as much of his free time together as possible; he was with me one afternoon in the autumn of 1940 – there was always a matinée and an early evening show at that time – when I turned up for work and found a notice in the back alley where the stage door was: 'Danger – time bomb'. Obviously there would be no show, but unfortunately I'd left some things in the dressing room – I had a little dressing room on the first floor, thoughtfully supplied with a glass roof. Nobody was supposed to enter the building, but I wanted my dressing gown, and Harry volunteered to go in and get it. I'm glad he did, because I kept it for years and *Applesauce* never did return to the Empire. The 'temporary' closure, during which the principals in the cast were spread around provincial Moss Empires (I went to Glasgow), became permanent when the Holborn Empire received a direct hit late one night. So the time bomb was really a blessing, because we had quickly got into the habit of spending whole nights in the Empire at the start of the raids. A passage went straight from the stage door to the dressing rooms; I would dress for the show, then come downstairs and sit about in the passageway every night, because I couldn't stay in my glass-roofed room. It was against the wall of this passage that we would sit far into the night when there was a warning on, and there, no doubt, we would all have been when the place was hit. Thus like too many other families, the cast of *Applesauce* was bombed out, and it remained homeless until the following March, when it reopened, with a few changes of cast, at the London Palladium.

As far as possible, entertainment generally was doing its best to offer business as usual and keep spirits up. When the war had started, there had been a general dither and everything, except radio, shut down completely. I think we must have been conditioned, by German propaganda and the newsreels of the fighting in Spain, to assume that the outbreak of war would be followed immediately by the destruction of most of our cities. Any activity that gathered large crowds of people in one place was automatically doomed. But when it was realized that it wasn't going to be like that, and that ordinary people were going to need entertainment more than they'd ever done in their lives, the industry pulled itself together, the theatres gradually re-opened, the hotels re-started their dances and there was a boom in the whole cheer-up business. By the time the war did eventually bring violence and death directly to civilians, carrying on in the face of it was seen as a small but significant act of defiance. And maybe the public had grown fatalistic: if Hitler was going to drop a bomb on you, he might as well catch you having a laugh in the stalls as hiding under the stairs.

Where the people couldn't get to entertainment, entertainment was now ready to go to them. In Britain itself a provincial tour would provide the opportunity. As a performer you'd do your shows in the late afternoons and evenings, and go to service camps, munitions factories, works canteens and hospitals in the area earlier in the day. The reception you got would leave you in no doubt that you were contributing something to the war effort. Which, along with thousands of fan letters, was what kept me going throughout the war: I felt I was doing something useful. For entertainment overseas, everything was done through ENSA – the Entertainment National Services Association. My turn for that would come later; for the time being I had plenty to do at home.

Away from live entertainment at theatres most people got their news from the Pathé Newsreels at the cinema, which were heavily controlled by the Ministry of Information. Newsreels were often edited to make it look as if we were doing better than we were: the most important thing was for them to put across a patriotic message that we were winning the war.

They also showed information films with practical advice about how to keep up the war effort (don't put more than five inches of water in your bath), about careless talk costing lives (watch how loudly you speak in public, as you never know who's listening) and about how to cope in an air raid.

Strangely enough, life in the recording studio went on more or less as usual. Although the faces in the orchestra kept changing, the routine for recording was much as it had always been; the difficulty occasionally lay in getting to the studios. One session for Decca at their West Hampstead studio had been booked for a nine o'clock start on a morning which just happened to follow a particularly heavy air raid. Because the raid had been such a bad one, I left Barking especially early and drove in towards Aldgate. There, it was complete chaos. Such buildings as were left standing seemed to be on fire; there were firemen, hosepipes and rubble everywhere, and the police were directing everybody away from the area. I was all on my own in the car, so I followed the rest and after a long detour through unrecognizable, shattered streets, I found myself back at Gardners Corner, the department store, in Aldgate again. So I tried to get help from one of the policemen, telling him that I had to go through the West End. 'I'm sorry but you'll have to go that way,' he said, pointing to the diversion. So off I went again, and I landed up, as before, at Aldgate. By this time I was beginning to think I'd gone crazy, so I tried once more, very carefully this time, looking to see where I'd gone wrong. For a third time I found myself back in Aldgate. I could feel myself getting hysterical. 'The only way you'll get to Hampstead,' said the policeman when I'd told him again of my problem, 'is by going out of London and round, and back through Stamford Hill.' So I did this long trip round the perimeter of London, and finally finished up at the Decca studio with only ten minutes of the session to go. My eyes were red and my voice was thick from the smoke and I was a bundle of nerves. But the orchestra had rehearsed the two numbers we were to do right down to the last dotted crotchet, and the engineer had got the balance all sorted out, so Harry Sarton, who was taking the session, suggested that I went in anyway and did a couple of takes. I sang both songs through once, and that was it. Both sides were released.

Important as recording was to me, for a large part of 1941 the Palladium was the centre of my world. It had been closed for some time by the Blitz when *Applesauce*, the refugee from the blitzed Holborn Empire brought it back to life in March 1941. The Palladium's re-opening was regarded by the press and public alike as a sign that the West End was determined to be as bright as it possibly could be in what had become very grim times. On 5 March, the new first night of *Applesauce*, Argyle Street – just off Oxford Circus – was as jammed with people as it would have been at a pre-war opening.

The show itself had been a fairly lavish production at the Empire, but it was enlarged and polished still further for its second incarnation at the Palladium. The production numbers were more elaborate, the spectacle greater and the costumes as gorgeous as wartime would allow. The reviewers seemed to have found a new term for the sort of entertainment it represented – they began calling it 'produced variety'; in other words it was still a variety bill but with sketches and other ambitious embellishments. The only major change in the cast as far as the principals were concerned was that Florence Desmond – the wonderful impressionist and singer – came on in place of Afrique. Before long 'Desi', as she was known, had become a great personal friend.

Life at the Palladium settled down into something approaching normality. Even air raids became routine. One time I got caught in a raid near Aldgate on my way home from work. I had to get out of the car and go down into the Underground because the bombers were coming over. But I found that I couldn't stand it down there: there were too many people, and it was so hot and packed. I went back up to the car and drove home, thinking, Well, if there is one up there for me, it will find me wherever I am.

We were often stuck in the Palladium itself, though, when there was a raid on. With the first house going on so early – about 4.15 p.m. – any warning would usually sound during the mid-evening second house. In my position as 'third top', as often as not I'd be just about coming on stage for my spot in the show when the sirens went, but by then we'd all become hardened to them. I think they just used to put an illuminated sign on at the side of the stage to say that there was an alert on, and I suppose there were always a few members of the audience who would get up and go, but most of them just stayed where they were and we'd carry on. Like everything else, it had its funny side, and you could more or less bet that if a bomb was going to drop anywhere near, it would be during the quietest part of 'A Nightingale Sang in

Berkeley Square'. But it became second nature to ignore it, and you'd take no more notice of a bomb going off than of a drummer falling off his stool. Desi reckoned that when the audience saw all of us getting on with our jobs they'd see no reason why they shouldn't stay and enjoy the show. Very often they would enjoy very much more than just the show, because if the raid was still on and at a noisy stage when the programme ended, most people would remain in the theatre and we would go on entertaining them informally. Some of them would come up on stage and we'd have a sing-song, until gradually they'd get tired and there'd be a lull and they would drift away and go home. Then the cast would be all be gone and I would be on my own except for the fire wardens, and we'd sit about and make ourselves as comfortable as we could until the all-clear went. If Harry had managed to get out of camp at Uxbridge he'd stay with me, drive back to Barking with me through the poor old battered East End and then go all the way back to Uxbridge. None of us got any proper sleep in those days.

One night about four months into the run of *Applesauce* I sang out of tune, loudly and publicly, for only the second time in my life. The first had been during my time with Ambrose. We were doing a stage show somewhere which had a number of sketches in it and included among its props a kind of joke bench, or form, built so as to collapse and unfold itself for a bit of slapstick. I was standing in the wings, waiting to go on, and so was this piece of trick furniture. I don't know whether something jogged it or if it did it of its own accord, but it suddenly went through its collapsing routine and a part of it swung down and hit me on the head. I was practically stunned, but at that moment the band struck up the opening chords of my first number and there was nothing for it but to go on. I remember trying so hard to walk straight, and hearing my voice coming out all out of tune and my struggling to control it. My hair was ruffled, I was swaying like a drunk and Ammy was glaring furiously at me. I battled on somehow, and when I came off he went for me until I managed to explain, as well as I could, that I'd been savaged by a seat.

This second, *Applesauce* occasion was much more serious, and I was out of the show for six weeks after it. I had kept up the gruelling round of twice-nightly performances, with charity shows and troop shows, Sunday concerts, recording sessions and occasional broadcasts fitted in between, often not getting much sleep at night, and I thought it was just overwork when I began to get as thin as a stick and feel generally unwell. Although I was eating like a horse, my weight kept dropping steadily as we passed midsummer. I used to have myself weighed regularly at the chemist in Argyle Street, near the front of the theatre, and the day I was down to seven stone I got really worried and decided that I must go to the doctor. I'd left it a bit late, for that night after the show I went back to Harry's mother's place in Stamford Hill, as I did quite often, and was violently sick all night. I thought it was food poisoning and Harry called the local doctor in. He examined me and said: 'You must be very careful or you will get appendicitis' – which I thought was rather strange, for surely you've either got appendicitis or you haven't. Whatever it was, I felt absolutely terrible and got Harry to telephone Mr Hutchinson, the manager of the Palladium, and tell him that I was ill and that I didn't think I'd be able to make it that night. He created an enormous fuss: 'She must come: there's a lot of people who've bought tickets to see her.' He just wouldn't hear of my being too ill. So I got ready, and Harry drove me to the theatre. Feeling like death, I got dressed and then went to Desi's dressing room and told her all about it. She was marvellous as usual, and made a fuss of me, and even gave me a nip of brandy in the hope that it might steady me. It was probably the last thing I should have had, but neither of us was to know that, and at least her sympathy and encouragement enabled me to face going on.

I used to come up through the floor inside a giant model of a radiogram; the doors of this thing would open and I would come tripping out on to the stage. Feeling really queasy by now, I clambered into this contraption and up it went with a sickening lurch, the doors opened and I prepared to step out. Ever since my juvenile days I'd had a tendency to run on to the stage. Both Desi and Wally Ridley had tried to break me of the habit. '*Walk* on, Vera,' Wally would say; 'just walk on.' 'Wally's getting his own way today,' I thought. I couldn't have run if I'd tried; all I could manage was a slow, almost tentative amble. My legs wouldn't do what I wanted them to, and neither would my voice. Somehow I got through one song and began a second. By now I was swaying all over the stage, and pretty soon somebody came and caught me more or less as I went down and I was carried off stage. They took me home after that and my own doctor came. It *was* appendicitis, and it wasn't much comfort to hear him say confidently: 'I've been expecting something like this for a long time.' Anyway, I was whipped off to the cottage hospital at Potters Bar and operated on straight away.

I was in hospital for two weeks that time, and feeling pretty groggy. Even worse than being out of the show, though, was wondering whether Harry and I would have to put off getting married. This was July, and the wedding had been set for 11 August 1941. I wasn't too sure of being well in time. It was Desi who helped. She had a farm out near Thaxted, in Essex, and invited me down there to convalesce. It was marvellous – out of wartime London, in the country again (the part of Essex around Thaxted hardly seems to be in the same county as the Thames-side places), with fresh air and good food. And, while I was still technically recovering, Harry and I quietly got married. It was a small affair – with maybe two dozen people, just family really, at Marylebone Register Office. Harry and my brother Roger both looked very smart in their RAF uniforms. I wore a white suit with a skirt that fell to just below the knee, a white pillbox hat and white lace-up flat shoes. We were almost late for the ceremony because we were waiting for a white gardenia which Harry had ordered for me specially from a florist's in the West End. We had decided it would only be immediate family because we had to do everything on rations, which meant we had only a few snacks and one bottle of champagne, which cost five pounds (it wasn't rationed, but five pounds was an awful lot of money in those days). Then we had a five-day honeymoon in a hotel in Paignton, making sure we took our ration books with us. They would take out your coupons for the food, you see.

Then it was back to the Palladium. After six weeks out of the show I was keen to get to work again, but I felt I ought to look different somehow. It was becoming more difficult for performers to look glamorous, and I knew it was important, because it was what people wanted to see. Someone asked me many years later if I used to draw lines down the backs of my legs with an eyebrow pencil and I'm pleased to say that it never came to that. I was lucky: I always had stockings, because as I was working in the West End I was allowed extra coupons for my costumes. I was always short of fabric for stage dresses as we couldn't get the silk that we had had before the war. Desi came to the rescue again by taking me to her dressmaker, Colin Beck, just off Bond Street. Up to then I'd been dressed by the Palladium, and always felt that I wasn't making the best of myself, though I could never quite decide what was amiss. Colin Beck came up with a beautiful pink dress which made me look plumper than I was – I was still agonizingly thin – and cost three pounds fifty and took fifty clothing coupons, a whole year's supply. It was worth it, though, just to feel so good in it. It became one of my favourites and two years later, as I prepared for my trip to Burma, although it was later reported that I took trunks full of ball gowns, it was actually the only dress that came with me.

I wanted some new material to go back to the show with, also. So I went to Wally Ridley, who got a whole pile of music down from the shelves and we spent a day going through it. I picked out three songs, one of which had started life ten years earlier as a Latin American number with Spanish words by

Augustin Rodriguez. The music was by Gonzalo Roig, and I think it had already had one set of English lyrics put to it but hadn't got anywhere. It was the English words of Jack Sherr that transformed it into 'Yours'. It was to give me my biggest success up to that time, and would inspire the title of what started as a rather humble little radio programme but turned out to be the most important thing I've ever done.

CHAPTER SEVEN

Sincerely Yours

That there was something about my voice which appealed to servicemen began to reveal itself quite early in the war, for in March 1940 my name appeared at the top of a list of favourite female vocalists sent in to a daily newspaper by the men of the Tank Corps. There was nothing unusual in the list itself, because popular music fans, then as now, were always drawing up their own championship tables just for the sheer fun of disagreeing with each other. As the list was confined to girl singers working in this country, this was a gratifying sign.

The real indication came in the next month, and was turned into a national news item by the *Daily Express*. Headed 'British Girl Wins BEF Radio Vote', it went on:

A plumber's daughter from East Ham – wide-eyed, open-faced Miss Vera Lynn – tops BEF singing popularity poll.

Bravo, Miss Lynn! Other tops were all American – Deanna Durbin, Judy Garland, Bing Crosby.

How do I know? Because three weeks ago the BBC's Mr Leslie Perowne asked the troops to tell him which records they'd

prefer him to play. And yesterday his compère, Mr John Glyn-
Jones, gave me the results.

Says Mr Glyn-Jones: It seems they want sentiment rather
than swing. Top tunes are 'Faithful for Ever', 'Somewhere in
France with You' and 'There's a Boy Coming Home on Leave'.

That was 17 April 1940. It didn't mean that from that
moment onwards I was 'the Forces' sweetheart' – my theatre
billings, after the fashion of the time, still had something along
the lines of 'Radio's Sweet Singer of Sweet Songs'. But the
Forces' sweetheart idea sprang directly from that BBC/BEF
poll and the publicity given to it by the *Daily Express.*

As the influential BBC producer of the time Leslie
Perowne explained it:

We'd done a type of request programme back in 1938, and this
was a Forces' version of that idea. Its audience consisted of men
of the British Expeditionary Force in France, and when we
asked them to express a preference, the cards came flooding in,
and Vera Lynn emerged as the clear favourite.

It established a link between the armed forces and me that is
unbroken to this day.

A lot of people have tried to work out over the years what
the appeal was, and I don't really know the answer myself. I
must say that a lot of play was made with the word 'sincerity',
which is very flattering as long as you remember what it means.
On the whole – and it was certainly true in 1941 – a popular
singer uses other people's words, and she hasn't necessarily been

through the experiences she's describing (in some cases the songwriter himself hasn't, either). So she has to use her imagination, which is not a matter of sincerity so much as conviction. The sincerity comes from the singer's belief that the words are right for what they are trying to say, that they are what she herself would use in those circumstances. If she can believe in the song, it doesn't matter how trite it is as a piece of literature: its message will come across. I can't do better than quote someone else again, this time an unnamed writer calling himself a 'middle-aged listener', who set down his thoughts about me in an issue of *Radio Times* in 1941. After recalling his own service in the previous war, and noticing the audience's reaction at a live broadcast I'd done from a troop concert, he said:

> *The words of her songs may have been so much sentimental twaddle. But she treated them with as much tenderness as though they were precious old folk songs, as though they meant something, something that she believed in and assumed that her audience believed in too … It may not have been great art. Who cares? I can only confess that if 25 years ago that young soldier of an earlier generation could have heard Vera Lynn singing to him – and as if to him alone – simply and sincerely, all the silly, insincere songs about home and the little steeple pointing to a star and the brighter world over the hill, that old war would have been made so much the less unhappy for him.*

I don't know who he was, but he had analysed with uncanny accuracy my approach to singing; he may even have told me things I hadn't yet discovered for myself, for I wasn't conscious of all the attributes he mentioned. I was working largely by instinct, and part of that instinct consisted – as it had done since I was a child – in recognizing what lay within my emotional and technical range.

The actual *sound* of my voice had been with me since childhood, too. Singing as I did came naturally to me, and as soon as I had become convinced that my voice really was distinctive I quite deliberately gave up listening too closely to other singers for fear of being influenced by them. When I eventually went to a singing coach, which must have been around this early wartime period, it was not to acquire a posh voice, but in the hope of increasing my range and allowing myself a wider selection of material. Wally Ridley recommended this woman and I went along to see her. She wanted a little demonstration, so I just sang, the way I always did.

'Oh,' she said, 'that's not your true voice, I'm sure.'

'Well, it's the only one I've ever sung with.'

'Haven't you got another voice? Can't you sing higher?'

'Well, I've got my bath voice, when I'm pretending to be in opera.' So I trilled away.

'Ah,' she said, beaming with triumphant satisfaction, 'that's the voice I shall train.'

'I'm sorry, that would be useless to me; I've got recording contracts for which I use my ordinary voice.'

'But that's not a true voice, that's a freak voice,' she said, appalled.

'Well, whether it's a freak voice or not, that's the one I've got and it's the one I'm sticking to, and if you can't help me, that's it!'

'Oh,' she said, 'it's against my principles to train a voice of *that* type.'

'Thank you very much,' I said, and that was the beginning and the end of my voice training.

So, what did I have? A voice which gave the impression of being higher than it actually was; arising from a need to have most songs transposed down into unusual keys – which automatically gave them a 'different' sound; a very accurate sense of pitch, which apparently I'd been born with; clear diction, which might have been my way of compensating for what I knew to be a rather cockney speaking voice; and a genuine respect for simple, sentimental lyrics, which I could sing as if I believed in them because I *did* believe in them.

'The Second World War was started by Vera Lynn's agent,' some comic cracked in the early seventies. That's one way of expressing that what I was doing, and the way I was doing it, just happened to be right for the time. When families and sometimes whole populations were scattered by war, the great uniting link was radio, while the simplest, most portable form of instant entertainment at that time was the gramophone record and the wind-up gramophone. Broadcasting and recording were my natural outlets; songs that spoke for very ordinary people were my chosen means of expression.

Requests for me to do specific songs over the air had been coming in from servicemen all over the world since early in the war. Some time in 1940, even before I went into *Applesauce*, I asked Howard Thomas, later head of Thames Television but then a BBC producer, if he'd consider giving me a fifteen-minute request show where I could do some of them. He said he liked the idea but then appeared to forget about it, for I didn't hear any more for some months. Then one night at the Palladium I was called to the stage-door telephone. It was Howard. He said, 'About that programme. We're going to do it. It won't be fifteen minutes but half an hour, and I've thought of a good idea for it. We'll do it in the form of a letter which you'll send the boys each week. We could call it "Sincerely Yours – Vera Lynn".'

The 'Yours' part of it was a neat touch, for I was back at the Palladium after my illness and 'Yours' was already showing signs of being a huge success. In fact it was one of three key songs of the wartime period. 'We'll Meet Again' was the optimistic one; 'Yours' was the love song and 'The White Cliffs of Dover' was the patriotic one – which I would record in 1942 after it was a huge hit in the US for Kay Kyser and covered that year too by Glenn Miller.

It was to be a modest programme, with a small budget and a small orchestra. Even if the money for a large orchestra had been available, it would have been quite wrong for the intimate atmosphere we hoped to create, and Howard's choice of Fred Hartley's little string orchestra was ideal. Fred Hartley was a lovely, quiet man, like his music. I'd already done some recording with him and I knew he'd bring exactly the light touch the programme needed.

The billing in *Radio Times* was as modest as the programme's ambitions: 'To the men of the Forces: a letter in words and music from Vera Lynn, accompanied by Fred Hartley and his Music'. The first one also included the words 'a sentimental presentation by Howard Thomas'. In view of what happened later the subsequent dropping of 'sentimental' is significant.

The first of the series went out in November 1941, a very grim point in the war. The Germans had almost reached Moscow; the fighting in the North African Desert was going badly for us; we didn't know it, but America was soon to be dragged into the war also. Although I didn't hear about it at the time, the programme did have some slight political intentions, in that the War Office had expressed concern at the pernicious influence that 'Lili Marlene', a German female voice using Lale Anderson's recording of the song 'Lili Marlene' as a signature tune, was having on the British troops, who used to tune in to her. Apparently she used to imply that the wives of British serving men were up to all sorts of things in return for black-market butter and meat while their men were away at the front. What was needed was our own patriotic radio antidote to this, it was felt. Howard could see no point in trying to counter one sexy, suggestive voice with another, and thought we should go completely the other way by using me in the role of a believable girl-next-door, big-sister, universal fiancée. But whatever the intentions of the series – nobody could have predicted its impact and success.

After the first programme there was such a flood of mail that we realized that we must have struck exactly the right note. More important still, I began to understand just how strong the radio link was. Although we did the programme from an ordinary studio – usually in Maida Vale, which had once been a skating rink, strangely enough – I had tried to imagine myself singing and talking from my own fireside, and addressing myself not to an audience in the conventional sense but to any number of scattered individuals. Since this seemed to have worked, it made sense to take it one step further and increase the contact by delivering more personal messages. So I had the idea of visiting hospitals where servicemen's wives had just had babies, and conveying the news over the airwaves to Gunner Smith, or whoever, within hours of the event. To be able to say to some poor boy serving out in Burma or North Africa, or somewhere at sea, that I'd actually been to see his wife and that I'd taken her some flowers and talked to her was like getting hold of their hands and putting them together. It used to make me sad that we could only choose and see and mention just a few, but I quickly found out that while it was marvellous for the handful of lucky ones, it was also reassuring for those who didn't get chosen, because they'd know that the contact was there. If the message was merely for someone they knew, even, it had the effect of reducing distances between people, of bringing them all a little closer. And it was here that the ordinary, commercial popular song came into its own as a greetings card. I was simply acting as a message carrier between separated people, and through the words of a song I told one what the other wanted to say. They may have quarrelled, they might have been shy, like most people – there was always a song that would convey what they couldn't say for themselves. The fact that I was myself a 24-year-old newly-wed with a husband serving in the RAF perhaps gave my voice even more authenticity. I certainly didn't have to 'act out' the words of these songs: they were close to my own heart.

The observation that 'It seems they want sentiment rather than swing' was still as true as it had been eighteen months earlier. For the most part I sang sentimental, wistful songs. They may have been the ones I was best at, but they were also the ones the troops asked for. But some assumed the customer, because he was in uniform and expected to be fighting for his country, in this instance to be wrong. George Nobbs, who wrote a very accurate piece about all this in a book called *The Wireless Stars*, unearthed a quote from the minutes of the BBC Board of Governors after the programme had been on a couple of weeks: '"Sincerely Yours" deplored, but popularity noted,' it said. The deploring was not confined to the BBC boardroom. Certain belligerent MPs and high-ranking retired military officers – none of whom was actually doing any of the fighting – jumped to the conclusion that a sentimental song produced sentimental soldiers, who would become home-sick and desert at the first catch in a crooner's voice. What the boys were presumed to need was more martial stuff – a view that completely overlooked the experience of a previous world war which, as it got grimmer, produced steadily more wistful songs. As I saw it, I was reminding the boys of what they were *really* fighting for, the precious personal connections rather than the ideologies and theories. MPs, an ex-minister and retired militarists fired off abuse at me and the programme, and the BBC – always ready to play the heavy father – set up an 'Anti-Slush committee' to try to protect the nation's moral fibre.

It wasn't done immediately, of course, for any kind of official move takes time, but under almost hysterical pressure from the hardliners, a committee was formed to deliberate regularly on what was and what was not fit to be broadcast to a nation at war. There was a particular faction at the BBC who considered it their duty to stamp out 'numbers which were slushy in sentiment', 'anaemic performances by male singers', 'insincere performances by female singers' and 'numbers based on tunes borrowed from the classics'. They claimed that singers like me – and songs like mine – served to undermine the war effort because they made the boys serving abroad more homesick. The only part of the ban that lasted any length of time, however, was the one on borrowed classics, but the anti-slush fight was quite fierce for a while. Some of the critics of my type of singing were very hurtful at the time, but it's amusing now to read of those old verbal battles and to think how silly it all was.

An enjoyable paper skirmish broke out, for example, between a newspaper radio critic calling himself 'Thermion' and *Melody Maker's* radio man, 'Mike'. 'Mike' turned out to be an unexpected and very persuasive ally:

> *The bulk of requests sent in by the members of the Eighth Army to the BBC's Overseas Service are for sentimental tunes, with recordings by Miss Vera Lynn specifically and predominantly asked for.*
>
> *And these requests are not from what 'Thermion' would have us believe is a 'Claque'. They are from ordinary serving soldiers who write in their hundreds ... asking for a particular tune that will give them some personal contact with home.*
>
> *I have yet to hear that the Eighth Army has in any way lost its efficiency on account of its penchant for sentimental music.*

Indeed the British seem to be doing just as well in this war ['Mike' was writing after the success at El Alamein in October and November 1942, one of the most decisive victories of the war] as their fathers did in the past with things like 'A Perfect Day', 'Roses of Picardy', 'A Long, Long Trail' and other songs which were anything but the 'virile and robust music' that 'Thermion' thinks the country is crying out for.

Soldiers get little time for trying to improve their musical taste, and in the middle of a war they like the music with the most direct appeal. That this music should be sentimental and nostalgic is just one of those things. German soldiers' songs are equally sentimental when they are not downright gloomy.

That the forces themselves didn't seem to think that their fighting strength was being sapped was obvious from the fact that they wrote to the programme (which ran not continuously but in several short series) at a rate of between one and two thousand letters a week. The mail came in from just about everywhere that British troops were involved. Mum handled most of it. I would read as many of the letters as I could, and those which needed answering would be answered; I'd sign photographs for those who wanted them. Where the letters seemed especially touching or sad, we'd make up a little parcel of cigarettes and any other small comforts we could lay our hands on, and send them off in reply. It wasn't much but at least it was a way of saying thank you to them for what they were doing for us. There was a bed named after me in one military hospital, and every so often there would be a letter from somebody different saying, 'I'm in your bed,' and we would send off a parcel to the new occupant. Often they would say, 'Next time you're on air, could you give a message to my mother or my wife ...' About half came from servicemen overseas; the other half came from their wives and mothers at home, wanting me to read out messages to their boys. It was a small thing, really, but it was all part of trying to keep in contact. By the end of the war I had sent tens of thousands of signed photographs and letters. What's sad is that I did not keep a single one of them. During the war there was a 'paper fund' and you had to contribute whatever you could to it, so I gave all the letters away. Although it was the patriotic thing to do at the time, it does seem a shame, as I would love to look at some of those letters again.

Just how seriously some people could take this form of contact I found out from a furious telephone call. The run of *Applesauce* had ended (I seem to remember that the show and *Sincerely Yours* only overlapped by a week or two) and I was doing an odd week's variety at the Coliseum. I was called to the stage-door telephone one day and there was a hysterical woman at the other end. 'What have you done with my husband?' she was screaming. 'He's gone, and I found this letter and a photograph of yours. You've taken him.' She babbled on, but when I could finally get a word in I just had to say to her: 'I send a thousand of those out each week.'

At the end of it all I don't know whether she was convinced or not, but I suppose her husband must have gone off somewhere – or more likely written to her, since he was presumably in the Forces, giving her the brush-off. Since I always signed letters and photographs myself, and never used a stamp of my signature, she must have believed that these things really were evidence of something going on. Although I felt sorry for her, I couldn't help taking it as something of a compliment that with all those letters going out, any one of them should seem truly personal. Even now my son-in-law, Tom, likes to joke that I should be careful how I phrase it when I talk about being busy 'entertaining the troops'.

When I look back now on this time, it is with increasing fondness and pride: I feel privileged that I was able to make some small difference. But it has taken a while for me to feel that way. Much later in my career – in the 1960s and 1970s, when I was doing a lot of television – I would occasionally get frustrated when people seemed to insist in thinking of me only in connection with the *Sincerely Yours* period, and in particular with those wartime radio broadcasts. But I see now this was the peak time of my professional life and a time of which I'm extremely proud of what I was able to contribute.

I never doubted for a moment that the campaign against sentimental songs was a load of nonsense; and I knew, without question, that if wistful songs could make some fighting man imagine for a while that he was nearer home, they couldn't be bad. But I had no idea until the war was all over what those programmes could mean to people who weren't even British, and who had no family ties with anyone here. *Sincerely Yours* was on the British Forces Broadcasting Services Programme and usually followed the postscript after the nine o'clock news on Sunday evening. All over Occupied Europe, individuals and small groups of people would be huddled in lofts and cellars and other hiding places, risking their lives by tuning in to the BBC to hear the news. Britain, they were encouraged to believe by the Nazis, was being bombed to blazes, and was near to collapse, but while the men and woman of the Resistance movements could hear the news from England they felt they were maintaining a link with reality. They would hear that people were still talking calmly in London. Then they'd stay tuned in and listen to my programme, and be convinced that things weren't as bad as the Germans were making out, because I was still sending messages, still singing songs. The knowledge that these things could continue to happen in our beleaguered country used to give them hope, they said. I'm almost glad that I didn't know at the time that there were Dutch and Belgian and Danish and Norwegian and other patriots endangering the safety of themselves and their families just for the sake of a few words in a foreign language; it was overwhelming enough to hear about it later.

I'm happy to have been around then, though, happy to have had some little contribution to make at what for us was the darkest moment in our recent history. It seems almost unfair that it should have worked to my personal advantage as well, but success breeds success in show business even more surely than in any other. Because of the fame – or if you were a member of the 'anti-slush' faction, the notoriety – of the broadcasts, in the callous terminology of the profession I had become a 'hot' property. How else can I explain my move to the cinema screen in 1942? Here's a girl riding high, they thought, so let's make some pictures. I loved the idea of this, but I also knew the limitations: I already had a reputation as

Vera Lynn the singer and knew that I would only really be able to play myself on screen.

Except for the awful business of having to get up so early in the morning, I certainly enjoyed the experience, and I loved the atmosphere of film making. I did three films altogether, one in each of the years 1942, 1943 and 1944, and for one of them Harry and I stayed at a little hotel near the Riverside studios in Hammersmith, London. Every morning we'd cycle to work along the towpath, across a little white-painted bridge and into the studios; apart from the fact that it was not much after six o'clock, it was very pleasant.

Make-up took the first couple of hours; otherwise I'd generally be on the set all day. Most of that time would be spent in sitting around watching everything else going on, because the actual shooting of the film was done in very short snatches. From the point of view of getting to know my part, that made it easy, for it was like learning four bars of a song at a time. It was the hanging about rather than the filming which was so tiring, and when I got back to the hotel again at around half past eight in the evening I was always exhausted. I'd have supper in bed, go over my lines for the next day (a waste of time, usually, since they were invariably changed when shooting began), put the light out soon after ten, and then get up next morning at six and start all over again.

I have mixed feelings about the films themselves. The first one was remotely based on some part of my own life, in that it was set in the London Blitz and was about a girl who, in the course of trying to promote her composer-boyfriend's career, is discovered to be a singer and becomes famous on the radio.

It was called 'We'll Meet Again', not surprisingly. BBC announcers were by that time well known to the public, and Alvar Lidell made a brief appearance in one studio scene. The music was provided by Geraldo, the big band leader, and his band, and the film did quite well at the box office. *Rhythm Serenade* came next; it was set partly in a war factory, a contrivance which gave ample opportunity for singing at a canteen concert. The plot was quite complicated and involved a temporarily blinded naval hero and a home for evacuated children. *One Exciting Night*, the last of the three, cast me as a singer but otherwise moved farther still from reality in getting me accidentally mixed up in a kidnap plot.

One of the problems was that I was just Vera Lynn; it was difficult for the film makers to take me out of that established character and get the public to accept me as another person. I was just *me*, it was hard for anyone to write a different kind of part. Today they would probably have found a way round it, for film makers seem to be far more resourceful now, though I'm forced to admit that the British have never been good at musicals. It's a great pity, for I enjoyed making the films, and I would love to have found a whole new career for myself in pictures.

But live stage appearances, recording and radio seem to have been what I was cut out for, and, not unnaturally, they too benefited from the success of *Sincerely Yours*. From the winter of 1941–42 I became more active than ever. Up to this point I had always been booked to appear on a variety bill by somebody else – an impresario or a promoter or a theatre management. But at this point in my career I began to do it myself. In other words, I would assemble the entire bill, take over the theatre for the week and assume the financial risk of success or failure. Both the rewards and the losses could be great, and since I am not by nature a gambler I don't think I'd have taken this step as soon as I did if it hadn't been for the rival bids of those two one-time friends, Bert Ambrose and Leslie McDonnell. Within what I seem to recall as the space of only a few days they both came to me with the suggestion that, for a salary they would guarantee, I should go round the halls as top of the bill in a show that they would put together and for which they would take the entire risk.

Leslie McDonnell, making a big deal of the terrible risks he'd be taking (every agent does this; it's expected of him, and he wouldn't be doing his job otherwise), suggested that I should go out topping the bill for £250 a week. After he'd gone I sat in my dressing room and had a tussle with myself, because I considered that I was lucky to have got as far as I had already, without thinking of going even farther. I was a little short of self-confidence, too, because, as I saw it, if I took Leslie up on his offer I'd be accepting a terrible responsibility. How could I risk carrying a whole show on somebody else's behalf? Suppose I failed? But before I'd had time to make up my mind one way or the other, Bert Ambrose, who had always dabbled in the management and agency side of the business, came along with an almost similar proposition of his own. That's odd, I thought; two of them after me. There must be something in it. Maybe I should have a go myself. I told Ammy about Leslie's offer, and he practically echoed my own thoughts. 'Don't do it,' he said, horrified.

'You can get much more than that. Don't you realize you're one of the hottest things there is?' (I told you the jargon sounded callous.) He went on: 'I'm willing to give you £500 no matter how big or small the audiences are. Don't do it; do it on your own rather.'

I didn't sleep that night, because I had to give Leslie an answer the next day. As the night wore on I became more and more convinced I would be a mug not to chance it on my own; I had this feeling that if I wasn't bold now I'd regret it for the rest of my life. If I go out on this first round, I thought to myself, and let somebody else take the cream, I'll never be independent. But how was I to tell Leslie McDonnell?

In the end I decided to appear rather more naïve than I really was. 'I don't think it would be right to accept your offer, Les,' I said to him next day. 'I'd feel the responsibility too much. Supposing I didn't make the £250; how do you think I'd feel? And on the other hand if there's a chance some weeks of making a little bit more I think I ought to take the gamble.' He went white, but he didn't say too much for fear of giving the whole thing away. He didn't do so badly from my decision anyway, for it was Leslie who booked all the acts.

So from then on all my variety appearances were under my own control, and I usually arranged things so that I would only work three weeks in four, leaving the fourth week free for recording, radio shows, charity performances and all those other things that artists are called on to do. The visits to hospitals and factories and airfields and army camps were still fitted in before and between shows, so this was possibly one of the busiest times of my whole life.

After a while, though, the entertaining life became almost routine. I know it sounds strange to say that during a war, but you just kept on going: you had to. It was hard work: I would go to the studios in the morning to make a record, and then I'd do a matinée and an evening performance at the theatre. What kept me going was that it was a job for me and I had been brought up to get on and work. And particularly during the war you were expected to adapt your lifestyle to fit with the times, however you could manage.

My mum and dad went on living in the house I had bought in Barking and after Harry and I got married we rented a house on the same road for £2.50 a week. At the time I was thinking that to buy a second house would not be a good investment: We've got one house on this road that might get bombed and we don't want another one, I thought to myself.

I kept on driving my Austin 10 all through the Blitz and often got caught in the blackout. There were times when I was performing at the Palladium and you would be stuck there all night waiting for a raid to finish. I had to drive myself because you just couldn't rely on the buses. You would put a metal plate over your headlights with a little pinhole in it so that you could see other drivers in the distance. It was unusual to have a car, though. Petrol was rationed, but I got extra rations because of entertaining – I was always having to get to the theatre or get to the hospitals on a Sunday to entertain some of the wounded boys. Sometimes there would be shrapnel coming through the roof. I used to carry a little tin helmet with me on the passenger seat. If I caught got in a raid, I just put it on and drove on.

I did let down my audience one night though. In the middle of a week's variety in April 1942 at Sunderland, the Sunderland Empire was closed for a night, without any explanation to the public. The reason was that I had been summoned to appear at a Royal Command Performance at Windsor Castle, and for security purposes the movements and whereabouts of the royal family were never disclosed in advance. So, thrilled and nervous, I came south and was met, along with the rest of the cast, by a coach at Marble Arch. The marvellous *ITMA* team was on the bill (from Tommy Handley's comedy radio programme *It's That Man Again*), and so were the husband-and-wife double act Nan Kenway and Douglas Young (who were both later to travel to Italy, India and Burma to entertain the troops), comedian Rob Wilton, actor Jack Warner (later known for *The Ladykillers* and *Dixon of Dock Green*) and the harmonica player and future star of *The Goon Show*, Max Geldray.

The occasion was the sixteenth birthday of the Queen, then Princess Elizabeth, a day on which Her Royal Highness also became a Colonel of the Grenadier Guards, and it was wonderful to stand looking down out of the windows of Windsor Castle on to the paved courtyard and watch the ceremony.

Naturally I was nervous before the actual performance, at about teatime, but perhaps not as nervous as I might have been if I'd had several weeks to get ready for it. I can't remember exactly how I got word that I was to go to Windsor – presumably through Leslie McDonnell – but the notice must have been very short, coming in the middle of a week's work like that. Anyway, I was suddenly taking part in my first Royal

Command Performance, and having my first close-up encounter with royalty. It was to be the first of dozens over the course of my life, and I went on to become particularly fond of the Queen Mother: although she was older than me (she was born in 1900, I was born in 1917) we shared a common history because of our lifelong association with the Blitz and our support of Second World War veterans. Princess Elizabeth was closer in age to me (seven years younger), but I always felt that the Queen Mother and I were from the same generation. We both knew what we and our country had lived through.

I discovered straight away at that first performance that our royal family are the kind of people you feel comfortable with. Particularly the Queen Mum – and the Queen Mother really did like to be called 'the Queen Mum'. When you met her it was like going into a room and feeling you were with somebody who was on your side, and who was interested in you, and pleased to see you. And when I walked on to the stage in front of her that day – it was quite a little stage in one of those lovely rooms – and she looked up and smiled in her warm fashion, I didn't feel nervous. In my experience the royal family just has this knack of making you feel at ease. The atmosphere that night was how it usually is with the royal family: very informal and relaxed.

I can't tell you what an honour it was to have been asked to entertain the future Queen for her birthday alongside the *It's That Man Again* gang, who were so popular then. At the time it was said that Princess Elizabeth's favourite song was 'Yours'. Out of all of my songs, it's probably my own favourite too. If Harry and I had a song during the war, that was it, because we spent so much time apart. Now, that's a song I have sung for so many different people but it was quite something to sing it for her that night.

It isn't merely because of that personal contact that I am in favour of royalty as an institution, though. It was part of my upbringing to be emphatically for the idea of a royal family: my grandmother was a great royalist and the whole family was unselfconsciously proud of being ruled from a throne by a figure it was our second nature to look up to. A country with a royal family is a different place altogether, like a household with a recognized, respected head. It sounds old-fashioned, I suppose, but to me, respect is the foundation of a stable way of life and the basis of a code of conduct.

If the visit to Windsor to perform for the royal family was sublime, what happened afterwards was faintly ridiculous. Harry was at Uxbridge, and we arranged to meet at Marble Arch on my way back, since that was where the coach was to drop us. The idea was that we would go together to the station and spend as much time as we could with each other until the train left to take me back up to Sunderland. I was a little worried the moment I arrived and found he wasn't there, because Harry was always punctual. I waited on the corner for a while; then to pass the time I went down in to the Monseigneur Cinema, which the BBC used at that time for overseas broadcasts, and where I was a familiar figure. Then I came out again and visited all the corners at Marble Arch in turn, just in case he'd gone to the wrong one. After that it was back to the Monseigneur, but when a couple of hours had gone by I became truly worried. I telephoned his unit, but he wasn't there, and in desperation I started to call the hospitals, because I felt sure that if he had said he'd be there he'd be there, and that only an accident could have kept him away. But the hospitals and the police hadn't found him, and in the end I simply had to give up, and I made my way reluctantly to King's Cross. Miserable as hell, I was having a cry all to myself at the station at about ten at night, when suddenly he was there in front of me. It turned out that he'd been at Marble Arch all the time: he'd simply started off at the wrong corner, and as each of us had moved from corner to corner so we'd kept missing each other. The blackout made it difficult to see more than a few yards and I suppose we could have gone on like that all night. I was so shaken up by it all that once he'd found me I didn't want to let him go, so we went back home to our rented house in Barking and I set off to return early next morning to Sunderland and my interrupted round of variety theatres, munition factories, hospitals and recording studios.

No doubt I could have gone on like that, but there was one thing I still hadn't done, and as time went by I became more and more acutely aware of where my next duty lay. For a long time I had been thinking to myself, I'd like to have the opportunity to see for myself how the boys are living. I ought to do my bit and entertain the troops overseas somewhere. You could only do that by joining ENSA – the Entertainment National Services Association, which had been set up, almost unofficially at first, by Basil Dean, whose headquarters were in the Theatre Royal. I don't think I could have had any idea, the morning I went up to his office in Drury Lane, what a journey I was about to embark upon.

CHAPTER EIGHT

Off to see the Burma Boys

It was only half my idea to go to Burma for five months.

'Where do you fancy going?' Basil Dean, the head of ENSA, asked me, when I told him I wanted to go overseas.

'Well, the troops in Italy and the Middle East don't seem to do too badly for entertainment, so if I'm going I'd like it to be where I can do the most good, where not many performers get to.'

'That's easy,' he said, 'Burma.'

As well as Noël Coward, the comic Stainless Stephen, music-hall duo Elsie and Doris Waters, and the comedian Joyce Grenfell, one or two others had been or were about to go to Burma, but that was about all.

'All right, I'll go to Burma, then.'

I had not travelled anywhere, really, before apart from one band visit to Holland. I certainly hadn't been in an aeroplane before. I don't even remember having a passport, although I suppose I must have done to have got to Holland. It seems extraordinary to me now but I don't know what Harry thought of me going – I never thought to ask him! By this point I had been married for little more than two years. I'm sure he didn't mind; and in any case he would not have stood in my way. In fact no one tried to dissuade me from going. Which does seem odd to me now, as anything could have happened and I didn't have a chaperone of any kind with me. I am still not quite sure what compelled me to go there, but I remember thinking very clearly that it was all very well doing radio programmes: what mattered was to go and sing in person. I thought it was my duty and I wanted to do my bit for the war effort.

There was only really one barrier to my going. Before I could go, of course, I had to clear my date sheet for those four months, which isn't as easy as it sounds. To any agent worth his salt it's an offence against nature to turn down work, and Leslie McDonnell was a very good agent. However, he quelled his professional instincts sufficiently to free me from all commercial engagements from March to June 1944, and the Burma idea became a reality. So, on 23 March, three days after my twenty-seventh birthday, I put on my ENSA uniform – a severely military-looking outfit along the lines of that of the ATS – and set off with my accompanist, the wonderful Len Edwards. If the uniform was practical, the pay was democratic and I think basic ENSA salaries fluctuated between ten and twenty pounds a week, no matter who you were. So that the sacrifice shouldn't be too great for him, I gave Len my salary during the trip. Whether that ever compensated for the physical and professional hardships he put up with, I don't know, but he was marvellous.

Because wartime modes of transport were strictly functional, some of the hardships began straight away. Nobody who's ever travelled in a troopship, or scrambled over the iron tailgate of an army truck, or flown in a military aircraft designed to carry anything but people, needs to be reminded of the agonies of just going anywhere at that time. Band coaches had seemed cramped enough after a few hours on the road, wartime train journeys had seemed comfortless and tedious at times, but all that was sheer luxury compared with the journeying Len and I were to do for the next few months.

We went first to somewhere on the coast – I don't remember where – and, soon after midnight the next night, took off for Gibraltar in a Sunderland flying boat. It was my first ever flight, and I didn't enjoy it. I was air-sick the whole time. It wasn't that I was nervous; it was just that I had an upset tummy. It was like going to sea for the first time, and the weather wasn't all that good. Because we couldn't fly direct across Occupied France and technically neutral Spain, the journey took us far out into the Atlantic and lasted seven long hours. We hung about when we arrived in Gibraltar all day, and I took the opportunity to send some parcels home and to buy some bananas, the first I'd seen since before the war. Then we were off again, at the apparently propitious hour of just after midnight. We stopped for an hour at Castel Benito in North Africa, for breakfast, and got to Cairo at half-past one.

Although I was tired and rather disorientated by it all, our hosts lost no time in whisking me off to see the Pyramids and the Sphinx. That was to be expected, I suppose, and I enjoyed it. It was what happened next day that was so wonderfully unlikely. It was Sunday, a day off, and the owner of the hotel we were in took Len Edwards and me to the races. Not only had I never been to a race meeting in my life before – and had therefore travelled several thousand miles to watch horses run for the first time – but I was also not a gambler. But in Cairo I backed four winners and won thirty bob.

I didn't see a lot of Cairo itself. We weren't able to stay in the top hotel of the day, Shepherd's, because of an 'infestation of creatures'. The thought of that still makes me chuckle now. So we were put in a small hotel. I had a single bedroom above a laundry and I was kept awake all night. All I could hear was 'tickety-bong, tickety-bong', with the washing going round. I asked if they could move me. So they billeted me with an Englishman I knew, a songwriter, who had his own bungalow. It wasn't ideal, but at least it wasn't as noisy.

This was where I first discovered what it was going to be like to perform. People wrote for years afterwards that I travelled with hundreds of glamorous costumes, but that wasn't true at all. I had taken one dress with me. It was my pink chiffon number which, as it turned out, would be very rarely used. I could only really wear it if I was performing indoors and most of my performances turned out to be in the open.

I went out into the desert at Cassassim to entertain 3,500 men of the Royal Artillery, just back from hard fighting in Italy. The plan had been to do it in the open air, but because of a heavy sandstorm I did three separate shows, using two marquees. With the whole place heaving and creaking in the wind, and the sand getting in everywhere like fog, I did one concert in the first marquee. Then I hurried through the sand in a jeep to the second marquee some distance away and did another concert there. Meanwhile the first marquee had been cleared of its audience and so finally I went back to that one and sang to the third batch of boys. They were a marvellous crowd and went to enormous lengths to show their appreciation. They'd even had a huge cake made with the words 'Welcome Vera' on it. They carried it in after the concerts, but it was immediately smothered in inches of sand and completely spoiled. It had its funny side, but it did seem rather sad after they'd gone to all that trouble.

I did some broadcasts while I was in Cairo, and managed to fit some shopping in – shoes, I remember – but it wasn't long before we set off again. Early one morning we climbed into what before the war had been an Empire flying boat, and took off towards the horizon as the sun rose. The weather was already bad when we crossed the Suez Canal, and we had to make a forced landing on the Dead Sea. Unless you suffer from both air-sickness and sea-sickness, you can't imagine the exquisite torture of a flying boat bobbing about on the waves. In one fell swoop it gives you the worst of both worlds. Mercifully, we took off again after about an hour, climbed over the mountains of what in those days was called the Transjordan, crossed the biscuit-coloured desert of Iraq and landed on the river Euphrates alongside the RAF station at Habbaniya. We had a short stop there and then we followed the river, a strip of dark green on the desert, down to Basra, just below the point where the Euphrates and the Tigris meet to form one great, wide, brown stream. They say the Garden of Eden was somewhere near where they join; you'd have to look hard to find it now.

Because of bad weather we were at Basra longer than we expected. We were woken at some terrible hour and told to get ready, but no sooner had we got up and dressed than we were sent back to bed again for an hour or so. When we did take off, we didn't get very far before being turned back. We finally spent the whole day there, eventually getting away in the evening, after doing an impromptu entertainment at a supply base (I believe Basra was one of the places that war materials used to go through on their way to Russia) and having a very pleasant dinner in Colonel Mole's mess. We worked our way down the Persian Gulf, touching down at Bahrain, and then Dubai, where we had tea and sandwiches, until finally we reached Karachi, where we were made very welcome in the mess of the Somerset Regiment.

We left the flying boat and continued next day by land plane, but there was no proper runway, and our Indian pilot hadn't been able to lift off before we got bogged down in loose sand. So we all piled out and waited for an hour while the aircraft's wheels were dug out. We got away in the middle of the afternoon and made Bombay at about half-past six in the evening. We stayed in the Taj Mahal Hotel, and almost the first people we ran into there were the two sister comedians Elsie and Doris Waters. Even in India, they were still simply Gert and Daisy; their stage act was them, they were just ordinary, nice people – the same there, all those thousands of miles away, as they would have been had I met them backstage at the Metropolitan, Edgware Road.

I got properly down to work, and during this brief stay in Bombay I did an open-air transit camp show, a concert at a nearby leave camp and a show at the YMCA. I also managed to fit in a visit to a hairdresser, long overdue, because up to then on the trip I'd been trying to do my hair myself and it had finished up by becoming a frizzy mess. And – a very personal pleasure for me – my friend from childhood, Leslie Day, now considerably changed from the boy soprano of Madame Harris's Kracker Kabaret Kids, spent a day with us.

Almost as bad as the air-sickness were the terrible early-morning starts, and our next move began at 5.00 a.m. We'd come right down to a Lockheed Hudson by then, which brought us, by way of Nagpar, to Calcutta, at two in the after-noon. On Good Friday I visited a large hospital, and it took literally hours to do so, because of course you've got to tour all the wards and sit on every bed and chat. It was here that I began to understand that maybe even more important than the singing and the music and the whole professional side of entertaining fighting men was this direct, individual contact. 'How are things at home?' – that question was the constant refrain of every hospital visit from then on, and you'd describe wartime London (or Sunderland or Glasgow or wherever you'd been that meant something to the questioner), and tell them that the shows were all running and that people were behaving as normally as they could. 'Business as usual' was not a sign of indifference to hardships elsewhere but a matter of pride.

Throughout the trip I was forbidden to write anything down in case it fell into the wrong hands. But I did keep a tiny burgundy Collins diary in which I would scrawl the odd note in pencil. It has lasted all these years and is now one of my most precious possessions – although I can hardly read a word in it: the writing has nearly vanished and I can't see so well to read it in any case. You only get a very small picture of what my journey was like and I wrote very little because I knew that I really should not have been writing at all. Thursday 23 March 1944: 'Left Paddington at 4.12 for Swindon. Arrived 6.30.' (This was the first day of the journey.) Monday 27 March 1944: 'Three shows. Returned through sandstorm.' Tuesday 28 March 1944: 'Went shopping. Bought varnish and shoes.' Tuesday 4 April 1944: 'Hairdresser.' (This must have been in Cairo.)

After Calcutta we did a show on a gun site somewhere; I made a few very cryptic notes in the diary, scribbling down the terse little message 'Lost piano, mike broke down, voice bad' – it sounded like a pretty disastrous day! The next day I had no voice at all, while poor Len went down with a kind of asthmatic attack and had to go into hospital for a short while. I was in a hotel, but I couldn't sleep for the bed bugs, which bit me just about all over, and for the fact that yet another hotel laundry was at the foot of a big shaft thing right outside my window, and made a noise all night. The next day was Sunday, and luckily there was no show. The day had its difficulties, however, because I was invited for cocktails at the Governor's residence, where I was clearly expected to entertain, but couldn't because my voice had gone. That night a very pleasant ENSA man, named Jack Bontemp, put me up in his bungalow, and I was spared the bed bugs and the all-night *dhobi* (the laundry).

While I was in Calcutta I was sent out with an ENSA concert party called *Smile Awhile*, but my first performance with them was also my last. Some of the cast seemed to so resent my coming out fresh from England that I could see it simply wouldn't work. Anyway, I didn't think it fair on them, as they had been slogging out there for a long time, so I thought it better to travel alone. There were more functions for me to perform in Calcutta anyway – including signing records for soldiers in a funny little record shop in a narrow alley. On the following day I was filmed for a newsreel, and I did a broadcast and then a live show. Another day I gave a concert at a convent hospital somewhere outside Calcutta and I can distinctly mention having to tread carefully because of snakes. Three performances a day – all in different places – was quite a common occurrence; what with the climate and the dashing about it was a hectic time, and I began to suffer the discomforts of prickly heat and those endless tummy upsets which seem to be an inevitable part of going anywhere east of Dagenham.

My real objective, of course, was Burma and the Forgotten Army – General Slim's 14th Army, which was now beginning the slow, enormous task of pushing the Japanese back. Finally we left Calcutta – with me sitting up with the pilot – in an aircraft that dropped mail at two points en route. That was fun, like going for a ride in the post van. We arrived at Chittagong, in modern-day Bangladesh, the last-but-one stage on the journey before Burma, at eleven in the morning. From Chittagong onwards I was firmly in the hands of the army and heading towards the front line.

I was to stay at the Officer's Club, and the first thing I did when I got there was to have a bath in a tin tub; there was no running water and my mind went back to the old hand-filled bath-in-the-kitchen at Ladysmith Avenue, which I had once had the nerve to think was too primitive for an up-and-coming young singer. In the afternoon I did a hospital visit, and made all the rounds, and then put on a show in a canteen. There was a terrific crowd; my brief note even says 'police needed'. Thursday 11 May 1944: 'Christened a large jeep.' Friday 12 May 1944: 'Open air concert. Pestered to death by insects.'

My shows took a predictable form: I performed all the popular songs of the day – 'We'll Meet Again', 'White Cliffs of Dover', 'You'll Never Know', a medley including 'Roll Out the Barrel', the favourite love song, 'Yours'. To be honest, the boys didn't care what I sang and I would sing plenty of songs which were not mine but which they knew – 'You'll Never Know', for example. 'If I Had My Way' always got a big laugh – they seemed to think that was very funny. Of course, I'm sure if they did have their way, they would have been thinking of something completely different … It makes me giggle now. It was all very innocent.

They were never what I would describe as rowdy. In general they were very respectful and I certainly never had a problem anywhere. Mostly the boys would sing along with me and enjoy themselves. They always seemed to be in good spirits, naturally pleased to see me. They would shout, 'How's London? How's everyone coping?' Some of them had been out there for years, since before the war started and hadn't seen home for six years. It was only when they were on their own with me that they would cry, asking me a lot of questions about life back home. You could see the tears come into their eyes as soon as they started talking about England. I remember one of them saying to me, 'England can't be that far away because you're here. It's like having a bit of home.' I became very moved myself a lot of the time: the boys were all so young – late teens, early twenties – most of them younger than me and they had been away from home such a very long time.

Some kind of pattern was beginning to emerge, in so far as Sunday was always *the* big day for purely social contact. I spent all of the next Sunday morning simply talking to the boys, and it really was moving to discover how pleased they were just at my being there. We did what everybody always does when friends drop in: we had tea and talked. The next day I appeared before about a thousand troops at the YMCA, signed hundreds of autographs and had never been so hot in my life. Then it was back for a quick wash and change to do a show for 600 officers. I don't think there were often separate shows for other ranks and officers, and I can only suppose there was something special about this for there to have been so many officers all in one place.

The fighting services were founded on the ideas of discipline and rank, and the first couple of rows of seats would normally have been reserved for the officers of the unit; usually that worked well enough. But at one concert – I forget now where it was – Len Edwards and I and the rest of the audience were all ready to begin, but the officers were late in arriving. I reasoned that if a group of officers couldn't obey the fundamental rules of punctuality, we might as well start without them, and I had the men who were standing at the back marched down to the front to fill the empty seats. I've no idea what happened to the officers, but the other ranks got their show.

Performances at various units to audiences ranging from a handful of men to a thousand or more followed each other in a bewildering succession; there was little to distinguish one event from another except that at a reinforcement camp I heard the awful yelping of jackals for the first time. Then one Wednesday we set off along the Arakan Road – which led into the hottest and most humid part of Burma – on what was to prove a terrible journey. The Arakan Road was a popular name for the Bazar-Teknaf Highway, where the British head-quarters were stationed. We now formed almost a self-contained unit: a driver, an officer or NCO, Len Edwards (with an enormous Smith & Wesson revolver on his hip) and me in one vehicle, and a small truck carrying a little upright piano, our microphones and our rudimentary public address system. We had to find somewhere to plug this in everywhere we went, usually into the headlights of vehicles. I needed some form of amplification; otherwise the boys would have just heard singing in the open air.

The first show we gave along the Arakan Road was at a hospital. Then we put on a performance for between three and four thousand of the lads at a rest camp. That was how it went: you never knew what sort of audience you would have, you just performed your best to whoever was in front of you. The largest audience I had was 6,000, the smallest I had was just two. Somewhere along this awful track ('road' was too good a name) we were met by General Slim's car, which I suppose must have accompanied us to Bawli Bazar. I know the journey in all took from half-past eight in the morning until five in the afternoon, and at some point along the way we did another two shows, one of them in a dressing station, for the front was not far away. I remember that well, as the boys had fixed up a little dressing room hut for me, complete with dressing table and bedecked with jungle flowers in a jam jar. Little things like that meant so much to me.

Recently an RAF type was recalling my trip down the Arakan Road and told me how they followed me on my journey, to see all was well. This I was completely unaware of. I also recall the time I was told on arriving for one show how the boys had walked for miles around completely equipped for battle, to sit patiently in rows waiting for the party to begin. They didn't know what time I would arrive but they were prepared to wait all day. At the end of it all my illicit and incomplete record says, understandably, 'to bed worn out'.

We started early the next morning again with a visit to a hospital, doing the complete round as usual, including an operating theatre, which was in a large tent. There an Indian soldier was having a bullet removed from his arm, and I pushed my way out of the flap on the far side so as not to be in the way. But they called me back. 'Would you like this for a souvenir?' the surgeon asked me, and handed me the bullet, complete with slivers of flesh on it. I still have it somewhere.

That sounds gruesome now but that sort of thing felt normal to me then. The truth is, before you go out somewhere like that, you have thoughts about what it must be like. You're close to war. You know you're not going to a town or a city. Or even the countryside. I knew exactly where the boys were — they were fighting in jungle land. I wasn't frightened, though, because I knew they would look after me. But it wasn't easy. It was hot, always so hot. There was nowhere to stay but in these grass huts, with two buckets inside – one for water, one for your toilet. I didn't think too much about it all; I just accepted what was there. I hadn't gone expecting to have running water or a bed to sleep in. I offered to go and you guess what it is going to be like. It was weeks before I had a bath. One night I slept on a stretcher balanced between two kitchen chairs in a shed. I found it quite funny at the time and I still do now. I had such a job keeping the mosquito net around me.

Mosquitoes were the worst thing for me – and the reason why I could hardly ever wear that sleeveless pink dress. In the open I had to wear long khaki trousers and shirts with long sleeves because the mosquitoes were so bad. If I was found walking around the camp with rolled-up sleeves, the boys would yell at me, 'Roll your sleeves down, Vera!' That's why in all the pictures from the time you can see me in my army fatigues. By now the hairdresser in Cairo was a distant memory and my hair was a mess. I just washed it and left it. There were no electric hairdryers. I had had a perm before I left, which in the end I don't think was a good idea because with the heat and the dampness it just went all frizzy. But it wasn't as if I felt that I needed to look especially glamorous. It took me every effort just to keep my lipstick on – you couldn't use other make-up at all because you would perspire so much that you'd have to mop it off. Lipstick was a godsend because at least it was something.

Not that anybody really cared in the middle of the Burmese jungle, where we were kept entertained by the sounds of elephants and heard jackals. We set off to appear at

Elephant Point, at the mouth of the Rangoon River but we nearly didn't make it because my pianist, Len, had forgotten the password. 'Quick, Len; think of it. You *must* think of it' – and I suppose eventually he did, for we performed there. Shortly after that we did a show at Ramu Airport for a very large audience – something like 5,000 boys altogether.

We zig-zagged back and forth a good deal, and then went back to Chittagong for more concerts there; and after that we seem to have gone to a place called Fenny, where I sang at a small mess right in the depths of the jungle. I had to borrow a pair of trousers from the Major, because all of my luggage had gone astray somewhere. I also did two shows in a *bashar* – a sort of bamboo hut with a dirt floor – the same sort of hut that I would often be accommodated in for the night. In the morning I'd wash simply by pouring a bucket of water over myself and letting the water drain away into the hard mud floor. What a world away from that tin bath in East Ham, I thought to myself!

CHAPTER NINE

A Journey with a Legacy

One of the pages in my secret diary of Burma has a list of words and phrases which I used in India and Burma whilst I was travelling. I have no idea what language they're in, but they came in handy at the time. Milk: *dood*. Sugar: *cheeny*. Water: *parnee*. Tea: *char*. I noted down all the numbers for one to ten and tried to learn them by heart. Even now I can remember asking for *parnee garrum* – hot water. I don't think I got it.

Now and again I would give the sort of performance I had thought I'd give when I was back at home, with an attempt at full hair and make-up. We did a lot of work around Fenny, and then moved to Comilla, where General Slim's headquarters were. Now part of Bangladesh, this was the frontier military base on the border with Burma and close to the front line. We gave some of our shows in something called the Town Hall. At last I could get out of the ENSA khaki drill and put on my pink dress. But it was so hot that, as the boys in the audience told me afterwards, this pale pink dress grew steadily darker as I sweated, until it was hanging from me, limp and sodden. I think that was the night I had some pictures taken with General Slim.

I met a lot of high-ranking officers during this trip, and strange to say I was less in awe of them then than I would be today. Then, everybody was doing a tough job of work, and they were just soldiers or airmen to me. It's only since that I've come to realize what exalted positions such people hold, and to feel somewhat inadequate in their company. I met Air Marshal Baldwin and later on Brigadier Lentaigne. He was the man who succeeded Brigadier Wingate, the man who organized the Special Force, which operated in unbelievable danger behind the Japanese in the jungle. Wingate christened his men 'Chindits', after a fabulous Burmese lion, but I don't think the name got into the official histories, because Wingate's unorthodox methods weren't too popular with most of the more conventional officers. I never met Wingate because he'd been killed in an air crash the day after I left England. But I did meet some of his Chindits, who emerged from a spell in the jungle while I was in Comilla. I was told I was to go and see them – 'but not today,' the message added, 'because they have to be de-loused and cleaned'. I didn't sing to them that time. For them, having been out of touch with even army-style civilization for months at a stretch, it was enough to know that the 14th Army they were part of was not completely forgotten, so we just talked.

Comilla was the centre of furious activity for me, and the round of hospital visits, and concerts for soldiers and airmen, sometimes in the open air, sometimes on improvised stages made of aero-engine crates (with the engines still inside them, in a few instances), have all run together in my mind in an almost continuous blur.

Every now and then something happened to make one particular occasion stand out, like the time I was presented with a bouquet of jungle flowers with surgical gauze as ribbons. By this time Len and I were in a state of almost continuous tiredness, but in spite of the discomforts we were so exhausted at the end of each day that we usually managed to sleep wherever we were put. At one point the piano suffered more than we did. After days of being jolted about in the back of the truck over those indescribable jungle roads, one night its case simply fell apart, and Len got through the concert with volunteers holding it together. That poor piano, it went through so much.

A visit to Sylhet (also now in Bangladesh) was memorable because of the extraordinary size of the beetles which flew clumsily straight into any lights that happened to be on, where they would stun themselves, drop like stones to the ground and then scrabble and scratch about on the floor, making an incredible amount of noise, that is those that didn't manage to get caught in my hair! It was at Sylhet, too, that I really was singing in the rain. We did the first of two concerts there one evening in the open air – it's not far from a place with one of the heaviest rainfalls in the world – and it started to pour down; I got drenched. We performed the second concert under cover somewhere, and it was there that I met Brigadier Lentaigne. Len and I were put in a concrete outhouse to sleep, with a sheet draped in between our beds for propriety. Tired as we were, we didn't get much sleep that night, because all of the time we had been having dinner with the Brigadier there had been torrential rain, and the rain came pouring in under the door of our outhouse (which was really just a shed) and we were flooded out. There was nowhere else to sleep, though, so we just had to put up with it.

We travelled from Sylhet to Shillong on a very dangerous and difficult road, some of it 6,000 feet up in the jungle-covered mountains. We didn't do any entertaining the evening we got there, but we made up for it in the next few days with performances at a Toc H convalescent home, at a garrison theatre, at an RAF camp and several hospitals. We also managed some relaxation there because, as I recall, Shillong's climate was rather more agreeable than that of most of the other places, and it was something of a rest centre for weary troops. We had tea with Mrs Slim there, and met Major-General Ranking. We also ran into Elsie and Doris Waters again, still imperturbably in their characters of Gert and Daisy.

Then the blur of travel and shows began again – Jorhat, an Engineers' mess, a hospital, a leopard skin given to me by a lieutenant, a Plantation Club audience of 2,000, a dinner somewhere where I was the only woman present; on to the Manipur Road; a show at a theatre somewhere, with many gatecrashers. Dimapur.

In Dimapur, near the Japanese border, I saw some Japanese prisoners. They were sitting on the ground, leaning against a *bashar* – they had obviously just been captured. They gave me a very curious look as if to say 'what is that woman doing here?' I didn't stop to tell them.

It was there, at Dimapur, that I visited three hospitals in one morning, and then did an afternoon and an evening show.

This was followed the next day by trips to two more hospitals. This was at the height of the Kohima battle, and the patients were all maimed, bad cases. The worst thing was the smell. Gangrene set in easily in those conditions and that was when I first saw an antibiotic being used, the early penicillin: it was in a yellow powder and they would put it straight on the wound. The wounded lay out in the heat with no sanitation in those tents. It was hard for everybody. The doctors looking after them were just boys themselves. I hardly ever saw any women and there were no female nurses in Burma. At one point, suddenly sickened by the smell of gangrene, disinfectants and the sense of desolation at the thought of life ebbing away all round me, I was overcome by it all, and sat down on some-body's bed, feeling weary and ill and futile. I asked for a glass of water. 'We've no drinking water,' someone said gently, 'but there's some lemonade if you'd like it.'

It was then that I thought of Annie Walker's well, nearly half a world away in Farnham. Sitting on that hospital bed, in the heat and humidity and stench, in my imagination I could see myself hauling up the bucket and scooping out a glassful of cool water which was itself as clear as glass. For a second I could even taste it. There was nothing in the whole world that I wanted more than that simple drink of water. While it lasted it was possibly the most agonizing, poignant moment in my whole life, with all of my childhood in it. They didn't know it, but those damaged men around me had all had something to do with making sure it would be there to go back to.

A show at a hospital, as distinct from just a visit, usually took the form of getting as many men as possible into one ward, dragging the piano in and singing. But always there would be men too ill to be moved, and I'd go and see them after the main performance was over. It was in that way that I sang to my smallest ever audience – of two. They were both too poorly to come and sit in the concert and were both terribly wounded. They asked me to sing 'We'll Meet Again'. I could see what they were thinking. In the end only one got home. Years later I was invited to do *This Is Your Life* and they had managed to find him. I never knew how: I didn't know his name and I certainly didn't know where he lived. I was so surprised and moved, I couldn't believe it.

It was at Dimapur that I fell in with two BBC correspondents, Dick Sharp and Jerry – whose surname I've since forgotten and have never been able to find. They wanted to take me up to the front line one morning and have me sing with the noise of battle in the background. We were too far away to hear the fighting, but they wanted their story. They said, 'We'll leave at dawn and go up the road. As soon as we can hear the guns going off, we want you to start singing. Are you game?' I said all right. Unfortunately some senior officer got wind of what was going on and stopped me. He said, 'You can't take that risk. She is a national institution.'

Dick and Jerry were marvellous company, though, and Dimapur is the place that still holds the most striking memories for me some sixty-five years later. This was the base for Kohima and it was where the real fighting was going on. Dimapur was on a river, and we stayed in a *bashar* behind a high wire fence by the water's edge. We'd take our meals on a sort of verandah, with the flies were so numerous that you just had to become indifferent to them. You'd get a bowl of some thickish soup, and the only way you could eat it was to get your spoon in quick and, with a sort of sideways movement, scoop it out from under the solid layer of flies which instantly settled on top of it. At night we'd tuck ourselves in under our mosquito nets and try not to watch the bush rats that ran about in the roof of the *bashar*.

Dick and Jerry somehow made light of all this, and in fact the only thing I ever heard them grumble about was that all they'd got to drink one night was a few bottles of mineral water, and they'd been weaned on stronger stuff than that. This amused me: you know journalists, they like their little drop. What can you do when you are with a couple of war correspondents and they are virtually panting because they are dying for a drink? Suddenly I remembered that back in Chittagong a somewhat fatherly officer had presented me with a bottle of Canadian Club whisky – 'Just a chota peg now and again for medicinal purposes, my dear,' he'd said – and that I'd been dragging it about all this time. The moment for medicinal application seemed to have arrived – in any case, apart from enjoying a glass of wine and the occasional aperitif, I've never been a drinker – I got it out from the depths of my luggage. Well, they couldn't believe their eyes when I came out of the grass hut with a bottle of whisky in my hand. We had nothing to put with it – no water, no ginger ale – so we had no choice but to drink it neat. The four of us – Len, Dick, Jerry and me – sat outside and worked our way peacefully through the bottle. I can just see us now, sitting outside these little grass huts with the river running in front of us and barbed wire all around, the battle going on up the road … At the end of it, inexperienced drinker that I was, I felt my way into my *bashar*, smiled benignly at the rats in the roof and fell deeply asleep.

It was around this time that we had dinner with a large signals unit, where I became aware of the kind of practical democracy the serving man likes to see. We had soya links (the infamous imitation sausages) and rice pudding – plain boiled rice with a dollop of anonymous red jam. I suddenly found that they were all surreptitiously looking to see if I was having the same as them. There wasn't anything else. At times like this I felt sad for the boys: they had so few luxuries. But what they did have they made the most of. I struggle now to remember very many meals from that time, as I suspect they were all so horrible that I would rather forget them. I was lucky that although I caught the odd tummy bug, I didn't get anything disastrous, and that I didn't lose any weight either, amazingly – I was very slim in those days in any case and there was nothing to lose. I visited one place and seeing a goat tethered to a post when I arrived. Later in the afternoon it had gone. I tried not to think about it but I have an idea they had 'killed the fatted calf', as it were, because I was there. It was a lonely existence, stuck out there in the middle of nowhere, and without the communications that they have today to make active service a little bit more bearable. I felt cut off myself: I could write to Harry, my husband, and receive letters. But it was not the same as phone calls and many of the letters would get lost. All the same, there was never a time when I wanted to go home. I had volunteered to do the job and I was willing to stay there as long as I was permitted.

We were near the end of our tour now. On Empire Day, 24 May, I was up at eight to pack, did two hospital shows before twelve o'clock and left at 1.30. We stopped over at Jorhat, where we stayed with the District Commissioner. Although we were up early next day to fly to Calcutta, we waited about all day for an aircraft because the weather was so bad. Finally, at about six in the evening, a small plane arrived, piloted by an American. Only a lunatic would fly, they told him, but he was determined to press on, as he had a date with a girlfriend, and as we were anxious to get back, now that we'd actually started on our return journey, we elected to go with him. While everybody at Jorhat shook their heads, Len and I climbed in and took off with the mad American. Between bouts of feeling sick I dozed, so I never really knew what danger we were in, but for an hour and a half we were completely lost. Every time I woke out of my doze Len would say, 'Nearly there,' but we weren't, of course. We eventually got to Calcutta at a quarter to midnight, with twenty minutes' fuel left. A journey that should have taken two and a half hours had taken us just about six. There were no seats in the aircraft, and all we had to sit on were some tin boxes. I felt terrible, but at least we'd made it.

From here it was very much the outward journey in reverse: Nagpur – Bombay – Karachi. There I met dear old Stainless Stephen – do you remember the way he used to *say* the punctuation in his sentences – and we went shopping together. Then westwards again, all the time to the accompaniment of signals and hints that something was stirring ahead of us. We passed very low over El Alamein so that we could see where the battle had been fought. It was at Djerba, in Tunisia, that the hints became rumours, and finally the rumours were confirmed. Tomorrow would be 6 June – D-Day. We left for Gibraltar, where I bought bananas to take home, and from this point on, with the air over Europe thick with activity, which no insignificant flight could be allowed to interfere with, timings had to be precise. Any mistakes in our timetable could hold us up for as much as a week. We were all anxious – anxious to know how the invasion of Europe would go now that at last it had started.

We got through on time, and I returned to England, after the greatest adventure of my life, to find that my country and its allies had embarked on their own greatest adventure. I couldn't help wondering if it would all be anticlimax from now on for me. 'Vera Lynn is back from the Burma battlefront, after entertaining the troops there, looking well but tired,' runs a newspaper cutting from early June 1944. If anything, the papers are usually guilty of exaggeration, but that word 'tired' must have been the understatement of my career. I was completely shattered, and felt that never again would I be able to get enough sleep to make up. But the quiet of Weybourne effected a cure. Auntie Maggie had left there by then, but the place was still full of friends, and Harry and I spent a couple of weeks in Mrs Higlet's little country semi-detached. The apparent permanence of Annie Walker and her cottage was comforting, too. Old Mr Walker had been born in it, and he intended to die there, which he did. It was that kind of place. It had no electricity, no water, no gas; nothing. There was a privy outside, and an acre of garden, and I doubt if there was ever a vegetable eaten in that cottage they hadn't grown themselves. Annie Walker – wonderfully named, for she was a typical Annie-Get-Your-Gun sort of lady – made her own wines using her own fruit and water from her only source of supply, that wonderful well. Her life was so regulated by natural things that she never had to wonder what she ought to do next. Unfortunately I did, and the time for wandering was coming round again. It was perhaps not so conscious a thing as that, really, because what I personally had to do next was obvious, since I had engagements to fulfil just as I had done before going away.

Sometimes I think that I never quite got over that period of my life. My memories of the wartime years are strongest when I think of Burma. And I find it difficult to imagine the young woman I was then: twenty-six years old, barely married, never travelled anywhere and suddenly in the middle of the jungle in Burma, a stone's throw from the fighting. It was a strange and wonderful experience that has lived with me for the rest of my life. And I have always carried with me the memory of all the brave men I met who were fighting that 'forgotten' war which made such a difference to our freedom.

Back in England, things seemed stranger than ever. I had been lucky so far that no one close to me had been killed or injured. The only casualty I had known well was Bobby Holland, my childhood friend from our Madame Harris days. When war broke out, he signed up for the air force and was killed as a Spitfire pilot in the Battle of Britain in autumn 1940. With every day I kept expecting to hear of someone else I knew becoming a casualty of war, as somehow the

England I returned to after Burma seemed more dangerous than ever.

The fighting in France was bitter, as everyone had expected, and very few people were neither unconnected with nor unaffected by the strenuous effort. Until then civilian life in England had at least been free from bombs and air battles and broken nights for some time, but I hadn't been back a week when the first flying bomb fell, miles off course, near Farnham in Surrey, and from then on the things came over like a horrible plague. It was the first time we'd ever been attacked by remote control, and this blind bombing of civilians became more inhuman than ever.

The V1s, or doodlebugs, were bombs with wings, an aeroplane with no pilot. In September the V2s started flying over: they were bigger than doodlebugs and more frightening, because you couldn't hear them until it was too late. In July 1944 I did a rehearsal with the great bandleader Glenn Miller for the first time: he was over here broadcasting and I did one of his broadcasts. All I can remember of him now is that he wasn't very friendly and didn't really have any conversation. He was just there conducting the band – very professionally, of course – and I went in, sang a couple of songs and had my photograph taken with him. He was very famous and it was a great honour to work with him. And it was the only time I worked with him. A few months later he was flying to Paris and his plane was lost, probably shot down. They never found him.

It was an unpleasant time, but it's funny what you get used to. You just accepted it and took each day as it came along. It wasn't as stressful as it sounds now. People had a black sense of humour about it. When I got back from Burma people used to say to me in jest, 'It was all quiet until you came home.' People had grown used to the feeling that you could get killed at any time, especially in London. It made me realize why I hadn't been scared to go to Burma in the first place: there were so many people killed in this country, at home. We were at war anyway, so what difference did it make where you were? I hadn't thought of it as being any more dangerous than staying at home, because it wasn't. When I returned home to the doodlebugs, this was truer than ever. In those days you didn't have to go away to war: it came to you.

CHAPTER TEN

A House is a Home

Things on the home front were changing fast. Harry, a long-time martyr to catarrhal and sinus problems, had been invalided out of the RAF the previous September after the discovery that he was suffering from polypi – little tentacle-like growths – in his nose. While they're not malignant, they make life extremely unpleasant, blocking the nasal passages and causing a good deal of pain, and they got so bad that he was given leave to have them operated on privately. The cure was only slightly less dreadful than the affliction, and it was a long time before Harry, now returned to civilian life, was anything like well again. And then, unexpectedly, the war itself took a hand.

It was at this late stage in the war that our own rented house in Upney Lane, Barking, was damaged. It had escaped the main blitz, but when a 'conventional' landmine fell very close to it in the summer of 1944 all the upper part became uninhabitable, so that whatever furniture survived was all crammed in downstairs; we'd been using the cellar as a shelter for a long time, and now that was the only really habitable part. Not that it was a bad cellar, mind you. David Land, who

199

later became a well-known impresario, helped us clear all the coal dust and stuff out of it, and we made it as comfortable as we could. We were actually in it the night a landmine fell in the next street, and I shall always remember an air-raid warden lifting the cellar flap and calling out: 'Are you all right down there?' Anyway, what was obvious was that we'd have to get out, if only temporarily. In the August I was doing a week at the Brighton Hippodrome, Harry was with me, and we thought we might look for a cottage or something in the area where we could store our furniture until we got straightened out in London.

That is how we came to acquire a twenty-two-roomed house perched halfway up the South Downs, with 198 acres of land, a view across the shallow trough of the Sussex Weald and two famous windmills on the hill behind it. The place was called Clayton Holt, and it sat on a ledge on the north-facing slope of the Downs just east of the village of Clayton. It wasn't exactly what you might call an impulse buy, although it was practically the first place we looked at. It had character, certainly, and it captivated us right away, but it also had possibilities for a new way of life together. Harry was just about still able to play, and was working at that time, with the dance band leader Eric Winstone. But after his illness and operation it made much more sense for him to live an outdoor life. Clayton Holt, with its 40 acres of productive land – including a 7-acre orchard containing 1,100 fruit trees – could surely be made to pay for itself and at the same time provide Harry with a strenuous but healthy new career as a market gardener.

And perhaps not just Harry. As the war moved into its final stages I felt that an era was coming to an end. I couldn't go on singing the wartime songs, and it would be a long time yet before nostalgia for them would set in and bring them back, if it ever did. In fact I don't think any of us recognized then that nostalgia was part of entertainment and that everything, but *everything*, comes round again in time. So I justifiably felt that there might not be much farther for me to go. Besides, I was past my middle twenties, and I wanted a family. Yes, Clayton Holt, for all its great size and doubtless enormous running costs, seemed to offer wonderful opportunities and a new start, now that we hoped the war would one day soon be behind us.

We moved in November 1944. It was pouring with rain and I had a streaming cold. As the day wore on and the parquet floors got muddier and muddier and the unheated house became colder and colder while the removal men tramped in and out, I felt steadily worse, and we got the local doctor round. 'The only place for you is bed,' he said, so we made up a bed on one of those convertible sofas in a small bedroom, and lit a fire. I think the house had been built somewhere around 1910, and it quickly became obvious that either the chimney had never been swept in all that time, or that particular fireplace had never been used and the chimney was full of old bird's nests. Within minutes you could hardly see across the room for smoke, and I had to get up again and move into the huge, cold main bedroom, which, measuring 28 feet square, soon became known as the Football Pitch.

Even through the misery of that moving-day cold, though, I loved the place. For years I'd revelled in second-hand shops, and although we'd come from a four-bedroomed house (which you could almost have fitted inside the panelled baronial hall of Clayton Holt) I quickly managed to furnish the seven bedrooms without any trouble. People didn't actually want big houses at the time, and, as large places were subdivided into smaller and smaller units, I suppose the big old furniture found its way into junkshops and auction rooms. It will give you an idea of the scale of Clayton Holt when I say that after we picked up, second-hand, a refectory table, what had been a perfectly adequate dining table in Barking was demoted to the status of a coffee table standing insignificantly in a bay window.

As you must have realized by now, I'm not a person for socializing, and you may wonder what was the point of all this space, all those bedrooms. Well, I love the idea of family, and for that purpose the house was never too large. When you've got seventeen people under one roof for five days at Christmas, as we did on at least one occasion, even the biggest place seems to shrink. And in spite of its size, the Holt was a friendly, welcoming building. I don't, for instance, ever remember the front door being locked. I suppose there must have been a key, though I don't recall seeing one. It would have been so enormous that you couldn't have carried it about with you anyway, so the door was always simply 'on the latch'. It was an enormous building, right enough, but it had the atmosphere of a small, much-loved, lived-in family house. Along with the house we acquired two cows – Sally and Betsy; four land girls; Mottram the head gardener and his son Bob; three other general hands; Wilson, who used to milk the cows; a 110-volt generator, which gave Wilson more trouble than the cows did; an ageing and inadequate heating system; and Roy.

Roy was a terrier, and as much part of the place as the generator and the boiler, even though he never set foot in the house itself. He was a tough, affectionate energetic little creature whose entire world was his kennel and the grounds of Clayton Holt. He caught rabbits (this was about eight or nine years before that dreadful epidemic of myxamotosis swept across the Downs) and chased foxes and raced to meet the car with a sort of crazy grin on his face.

For nearly a year I continued working more or less normally. Travelling wasn't difficult from that part of Sussex, so – having picked up again from where I had left off when I went to Burma – my professional life went on unchanged. There was a little unpleasantness in 1944 when I tried to get some kind of curb put on the more spiteful impersonations of me, and for a short while there was a lot of misunderstanding. All performers are fair game for impersonators (and don't forget that one of my closest friends in the business, the actress and comedienne Florence Desmond, was famous for her brilliant impressions), and at one level imitation really is a sincere form of flattery, but the amount of envious malice that was going into some impersonations of me seemed to me to be unreasonable. More than that, I believed they'd taken ridicule to the point where it could actually harm me, and I tried to do something about it. Legally it was a difficult point to make, but through statements in the press and replies to criticisms I tried to express my annoyance that they were mocking what I believed passionately to have been important work, and that by descending to spite they were undermining my ability to make a living. I had seen the singer Jessie Matthews suffer in this way (she was lampooned for sounding 'too posh'), and I didn't want it to happen to me. Mercifully, my reputation seems to have been more durable than the ridicule, and most people have even forgotten that the episode ever occurred.

In any case, I soon had something else to think about. I was pregnant. Even before I collapsed on stage at Sheffield in the autumn of 1945, I had decided to retire when our baby was born. As I said, there was a feeling that an era was passing of which I had been very much a part; and since I never, in spite of everything, had been exclusively career minded, this seemed a good time to leave it all. We had been putting off starting a family ever since our wedding in August 1941, as it didn't seem to be the right thing to do to have a baby with the war still on and especially with the plans I had to travel to entertain the troops. But by mid-1945 – even before victory in Europe in May and VJ Day in September – it felt as if the war was ending and I was ready to become a mother. I didn't make any kind of official announcement, though: I wanted to see how I felt when the baby came.

Virginia Penelope Ann was born in a Hove nursing home on 10 March 1946. She likes to joke that she was named after a brand of tobacco and in a roundabout way she was. We intended to call her Penelope Ann, but Harry smoked at the time and he noticed someone with a tin of Golden Virginia (he smoked Camels himself). So when he came in to visit he had this idea that he wanted to name her Virginia. Fortunately I liked the name too.

With my love for the area around Farnham you may wonder why we hadn't chosen to move out there somewhere, making our family a Farnham one. I nearly did, once. Back in 1938, when I knew the time had come to leave East Ham, I'd actually got as far as looking at some houses on the Surrey/Hampshire border. My mother's intense dislike of being 'shut away' in the country, and one or two practical considerations, made me decide against it in the end. But it was easy enough to feel 'local' to the hinterland of Brighton. After all, Harry had proposed to me there, and we had now found a house in that part of the world which I loved enough to want to put my roots down there; I was very happy for Virginia to be a Sussex child.

Virginia seemed pretty pleased about it, too; from the first she hated to be indoors if there was a chance to be outside. She would lie in her pram for hours, watching the robins that perched on the pram handle, delighted with the movement of the trees. And not just in fine weather. As that bitter winter of 1946–47 set in, she would still prefer to be outside; only on the very worst days would she be brought indoors, and even then she was fretful unless she was parked by an open window.

This wasn't just an obsession on my part about fresh air; there was a very practical reason as well. One day we put her into that small bedroom I'd retreated to the day we had moved in. Since the chimney didn't draw properly, we had had an oil heater put in there, and on this occasion something went wrong with it and it smoked. Virginia was in her cot, and we discovered the whole place covered in a layer of black, greasy soot – Virginia included. I don't know to this day what saved her from suffocating.

For all their rigours and inconvenience, it's the winters at Clayton Holt I remember best. I think it's because they were so uncompromising. When it was cold, it was extremely cold; when it was bleak, it was enormously bleak; when it was beautiful, it was breathtaking. One morning I got up to the most fantastic sight of my whole life. On the north slope of the Downs, away from any softening influence the sea might have had, and high enough up the hillside to catch every breath of north and north-easterly wind, the place could be plunged into really low temperatures. On this particular morning I suppose there had been rain followed by sudden, severe frost, for all the trees appeared to be covered in thin glass. It was as if a giant had dipped them in water and quick-frozen them, so that every twig was perfectly encased in ice. The sun was just coming up and its rather pale light caught the glazed trees so that the view from the window was a tangle of stark, black, dead wood and sharp splinters of cold white light. It was worth being at Clayton Holt just for that one moment.

The central heating system was old and primitive and wasteful, and in the course of a winter would use up enough fuel to have taken the *Queen Mary* on a round trip across the Atlantic; in any case, its almost useless efforts were largely directed towards keeping the greenhouses above freezing point. But there was plenty of timber, so there was always the fragrant compensation of great log fires. We chopped our own wood, of course, and I had my own small axe, which was as much part of my equipment at Clayton Holt as my thimble was. Harry was the chief family lumberjack, however, and developed a taste for chopping, sawing and shifting wood that never left him.

One year we cut our own Christmas tree from the grounds, and from Clayton Holt's enormous entrance hall it rose magnificently up through two floors – you could do things on that scale there. The member of the Pierpoint Morgan family who had built it early in the twentieth century had found it necessary to have a whole section of the hillside levelled to accommodate it. The cultivated part of the garden behind it was on a steep rise broken by terraced lawns and paths. One group of rooms formed almost a separate suite, including a little boudoir with a balcony outside. From here you were only slightly above the level of the top lawn with its beautiful urns and statuary. Then there was an avenue of trees and a few more steps up to another smaller lawn, which really was at eye level. It was here that foxes and their cubs used to emerge from some 40 acres of surrounding woods and play within full sight of our windows.

The house brought out the marked difference in attitude to life between my mother and my father. Mum thought the whole scheme was harebrained – not just the attempt to become self-supporting smallholders, but living in that kind of district at all. The Sussex Downs, and on the side *away* from Brighton at that, were the very essence of what she meant by 'shutting yourself away' (and there were plenty of other people who took the same attitude as Mum). We could never make her understand that it wasn't a lonely place, that out of every window there was something to see, that if you looked northwards across the low-lying ground towards Hassocks and

Haywards Heath and Ditchling Common, there were houses and cottages and things moving along the roads, and that there was no more loneliness here than in many a suburban street. But Dad loved it. 'Oh, lovely, mate,' was his warm comment on the house, and he was in favour of everything we did. He was naïvely delighted that his daughter could live in a house that he unashamedly thought very grand, but his fondness for it was not solely due to its size: he sensed its intimate qualities as a place to live in as well, and liked everything about it.

And we made local friends, too. Adaptable, as I think most show-business people are, we were also ordinary and unsophisticated, and the visitors who came up and enjoyed an evening with us in our lovely billiard room were more likely to be the local butcher, the local fishmonger, greengrocer and doctor and garage man than any imported acquaintances.

If Clayton Holt was a success as a home, unfortunately it was a failure as a business enterprise. Even then, not counting Harry's and my inexperience, labour was a problem. Agricultural wages were low; 'two pound ten a week and all the milk you could drink' was the way Harry described it, and he may not have been far wrong, but it still wasn't easy to find enough people willing to do the hard work the place demanded. Always we had some good hands, but never a full complement. The sheer size of the house made extra difficulties, of course, because when I was working, or later on looking after Virginia, it was far too much for me on my own and we always had to have somebody to help. Of the couples who came to live in, so often it was a case of one being marvellous and the other being useless, with the result that they practically cancelled each other out.

It may be that we were too green to take on such a life, but whatever sheer hard work we could do we did. In the spring we even put our one natural crop to work for us by gathering the thousands of daffodils that grew in the sheltered parts of the grounds and bundling them up in dozens for sale. We sold the surplus milk from the two cows to a nearby farm; we raised what seemed to be tons of salad stuff, only to find that a lettuce we'd grown, picked, packed and delivered would earn us a farthing, yet be offered for sale in Brighton for one-and-six. We kept chickens, we grew soft fruit, we tended the orchards. The enormous boiler swallowed fuel voraciously and roared like a volcano but produced remarkably little heat. I still don't know where exactly we went wrong, but soon we had to admit to ourselves that there wasn't anything in it. Having got that far, our course became clear: I would have to abandon my hopes of complete retirement and go back to work; and we would have to leave Clayton Holt.

A return to work was probably inevitable for me at some time or other, if only – as Decca gently reminded me – because I had a recording contract to fulfil. And, as we discussed, if either of us went back to music, it would have to be me, for – assuming the public still wanted me at all – I would be able to earn more as a singer than Harry would as an instrumentalist, and that was important, as by now Clayton Holt had become an expensive luxury.

Eaten up with nerves, I went back to the variety stage, for the first time since I had collapsed whilst pregnant, at the

Chiswick Empire in February 1947. Virginia wasn't yet a year old. It was the coldest winter in living memory, and at the end of that first week, relieved that the public had not forgotten me, I drove back to Sussex with Harry through heavy snow. Considering how bad the weather was, we did fairly well all the way to Clayton itself. Then, at a steep hill by the waterworks on the lane leading up from the village, we got stuck in a huge drift. We got out and slogged the rest of the way knee-deep through the snow. Unfortunately, Clayton Holt had a long, steep drive up through the trees, so that when we got to the gate we still had a way to go. Slipping and stumbling in the dark, we finally fell in to the house, tired and cold and wet, to find that my dad, who was visiting, had stayed up to welcome us. He'd got a big roaring fire going in the hall, and the light from it flickered and winked on the panelling and the chandelier, on the oak staircase and the huge portraits of people whose names I never did find out. 'Cor, mate!' he said. 'Come in; you must be frozen. I've got a nice fire, though.' So we sat round the burning logs, a bit like the field mice in *The Wind in the Willows*, and took our soaking wet shoes and stockings off. We had some whisky to warm us up, and while we were sitting there sipping it and coughing and getting our breath back, Dad came staggering in again carrying a great zinc bath of hot water, which he set down on the hearth. And then, in front of the huge fireplace, with its carved surround of dark wood, we dangled our feet in the hot water and slowly came back to life.

It was almost the last great moment in that house, for we left it in March of that year to go and live in a flat near Regent's Park. This was a move for purely practical reasons.

From the point of view of my resumed profession it was central, it was convenient, it was functional, but I didn't love it. It was a big flat, and as flats go it was a good one; Virginia's garden became Regent's Park, but a park isn't the country or indeed a 'real' garden, and I very soon got browned off with it. I schooled myself to endure it by doing what I always do when I've had to leave a place I've been fond of – I dwelled upon the inconveniences and impossibilities of Clayton Holt and tried to forget its far more numerous good points. And yet the place asserted itself, for I've never stopped having dreams about it. In that strange way of dreams, the house in my mind's eye is never exactly the Holt, though I know it's meant to be. Ironically, considering how we'd loved it, it proved remarkably difficult to sell. It didn't make its reserve price when it was put up for auction, and it stood empty for several months after our retreat to Regent's Park. By then we were just about ready to make our next move – to Finchley.

Two things sold the house in Finchley to us: the garden, which for a house so close to town was enormous, and the extra room somebody had built on to it. Its original purpose had been as a sort of children's playroom, and compared with the rest of the rooms, which were quite modest in size, it was big. Big enough in fact to take the grand piano and become an ideal music room. That made it perfect, but oddly enough we nearly didn't take it, because the surveyor's report was full of ominous references to dry rot. The year 1949 wasn't a good one for getting timber for domestic building or, come to that, getting builders to do domestic jobs, and we carried on looking. But after a few months we'd found nothing to equal it, and the agent came back and said the house was still on offer and that the dry rot had been seen to as far as possible. So, resigning ourselves to the idea that most houses have some rot in them somewhere, and that we might get a few years' peace and comfort before the floors fell in, we decided to risk it after all. We were there for twenty-two years.

It was not simply a convenient place for town, for Virginia's school and for my work (though it was especially that; it's surprising the difference living on the north side of London can make if you've got to go to Blackpool or Leeds in a hurry). It was also another of those friendly, welcoming houses, and it became the setting for fabulous family parties. It's not too much to say that we became famous for our Boxing Day and New Year's Eve parties, and there was always some family anniversary to celebrate.

But Finchley still wasn't the country, and it was not long before I felt the need to have some country place to escape to – especially since, contrary to all my fears, I was soon doing more work than ever. So we found a small cottage called Three Beams in Ditchling, not far from Clayton. There, opposite the village pond and within sight of the little old church perched up on its mound, we began – at weekends and whenever we could get away – our association with the village which is now our real home, the place in whose community we like to think we belong. That I could increase my foothold in Ditchling, so to speak, to the point where I now have a house there, which I designed myself and which is my permanent home, I owe to what amounts almost to a second career.

CHAPTER ELEVEN

After the Interval

Going back to work in February 1947 had been like having to begin again – twice over. The agony of nervousness I suffered was bad enough, but this time, as well as facing my first audience for over eighteen months, I was going to find out, perhaps once and for all, whether people still wanted me.

That I had a faithful record public appeared fairly certain, for my contract with Decca was still in force and I had done some recording even when Virginia was tiny. There was a record called 'Our Baby' which obviously comes from that time; and for 'I'm Happy for Your Sake' and 'The World Belongs to You, Little Man,' released in January 1947, as I think they were, means that I was back in the studio by the tail end of 1946. But recording was never such a nerve-wracking experience; how you dressed was unimportant, you could have the words stuck up in front of you and you could concentrate exclusively on the interpretation of the song. The variety stage involved direct contact with the audience, then and there. Everything had to be right, you couldn't stop and start again, and reaction was immediate. In fact reaction began even before you sang a note, for your name and reputation had to bring the people in to start with.

To my great joy the public seemed pleased to see me once more, and several papers had variations on the theme of 'welcome back to a new-old favourite'. It seemed that people were still living ordinary lives and they still wanted hope and comfort. Outwardly, little had changed. The variety theatres, apart from those destroyed or badly damaged in the war, were still going strong, for television had only started up again in the summer of 1946, and hadn't yet shown what a force it could be.

It was to be some time before music hall and variety would die completely: it wasn't until 1957 that John Osborne said in *The Entertainer*, 'The music hall is dying, and with it, a significant part of England.' Competition from television and popular music eventually killed it off, especially when rock and roll came in, and within a few years of the war ending this unique breed of live entertainment which had given us Flanagan and Allen, George Formby, Gracie Fields and Max Miller was on its last legs.

Radio was still king in the post-war period, however, and within a few weeks of going back to variety I was on the air with my own series again, once again entitled *Sincerely Yours* and once again reaching out to servicemen overseas. This was a particular pleasure for me, since I was able to insist – and I had it in writing before I would sign – that the musical director was Bob Farnon, the brilliant Canadian conductor/composer/arranger who'd come over here with the Canadian band of the American Expeditionary Force and, luckily for us,

Left: In costume in
We'll Meet Again,
1943.

Above: Behind the scenes filming *We'll Meet Again*.

Right: Entertaining the troops in Burma.

Below: Visiting wounded soldiers in a field hospital in Burma.

Above: With field nurses at a station in India.

Above: Singing to the troops under an awning – a makeshift stage!

Above: On a rickshaw pulled by my pianist, Len Edwards.

Above: Being fitted for a wonderful outfit for *London Laughs* – Virginia looks very impressed!

Above: London Laughs with Tony Hancock and Jimmy Edwards.

Above: With the Not Forgotten Association, 1950.

Right: In 1950 with my daughter Virginia.

Above: Rehearsing for the Royal Variety in 1960 with Liberace – the girls are myself, Marion Ryan, Alma Cogan, Janette Scott, Yana and Anne Shelton.

Right: Performing on stage in 1970.

Left: Receiving the Burma Star Award in 1985 from Air Vice Marshal Sir Bernard Chacksfield, then chairman of the Burma Star Association.

Above: With Harry, meeting the Queen Mother.

Above: With Harry, 1994.

decided to stay. These programmes were completely different from my wartime broadcasts, more like good general light-music shows, and before the first series was over I was tickled pink to find that they were second in popularity only to that old comedy favourite *It's That Man Again*.

My working life began to have a very familiar look about it except for one thing. If I had retired completely, it would have been to devote myself to being a mother; now that circumstances had brought me back, I was still going to be as much of a mother as I could. Harry, Virginia and I began to travel as a family. We took a girl with us, a nanny, to babysit in the hotel room during the evenings, and toured Britain as a family unit. I could have left Virginia at home in somebody's no-doubt expert care, but I wanted to bring her up myself as much as possible. Even when we'd lived a life of hard physical work at Clayton Holt, anyone I'd had in to help look after the baby had never done more than just that. I fed her, bathed her and put her to bed; I wasn't going to have any of that nonsense where the nanny produces a spotless infant at around teatime for a kiss and a smile and then whisks her away again to some distant part of the house. Virginia was mine, mine and Harry's, and she belonged right where we were, first in a cot in our bedroom, and later in the nursery next door. After we moved, and until it was time for her to go to school, she might just as well come with us on tour.

On the whole she was a good child, and I began a policy then of being strictly honest with her. Some nights, when it was time for me to go off to work, she would cry and not want me to go. One of the women we had to look after her at night advised me not to let her see me go; she wanted me to go by stealth, just to keep the peace. But I wouldn't. From the moment Virginia was old enough to understand, I used to tell her that I was going to work and that I'd see her in the morning. It didn't matter how much she cried; she had to get it into her head that I was going out, and that I would keep my promise – if I said I would be back, I would be back. Also (and this seemed to me to be very important), I wanted her to know why I wouldn't be there at certain times; there's nothing worse than for a child to wake up in the middle of the evening and not find the people she expects to be there, and not know why they're not there. If she sees you go, she understands.

That we were a complete family was made possible by the way Harry's role was subtly changing. After the operation which had taken him out of the Squadronnaires, he had made one or two minor sorties into music, including, for a time, fronting a trio. But the attitude of the period was strange, and there was a marked reluctance on the part of leaders or managers to use him, on the grounds that I was doing pretty well, so what did he want a job for? I could never see the logic behind that, but it meant that it made sense for him to start coming around with me, to start learning the business – the working of a theatre, the lights, the sound, the travelling arrangements and all the rest of it. He gradually transformed himself into my indispensable personal manager, the scourge of lighting men and sound men, ensuring that everything was as right as it could be for the presentation of my act. In a television interview in 1975, Michael Barrett complained in a good-natured but puzzled way that whenever he tried to reach me by phone it was always Harry who answered and he always said, 'What do you want her for?' Well, of course. Harry organized things so that all I had to do was sing the songs.

And in the late forties it looked as though I was going to be allowed to sing the songs much as I had always done. The business as a whole, however, was facing changes far more profound than the fluctuations of any individual performer's personal fortunes. Television gradually showed its strength, and the variety circuits, which had enabled even the humblest artist to do some kind of work for maybe forty-eight weeks in the year, began to shrink. And the nature of the once-innocent acts began to change. This was the period when somebody's Naughty Nudes would appear on the number-two circuit halls, or when you'd find, say, the Camberwell Palace putting on shows with titles like *Nine O'Clock Nudes* or *Nudes of all Nations*. It was funny in a way, but sad also, because no matter how attractive the girls might have been (and often they weren't), we were helplessly witnessing a great institution in decline, for all too frequently the next stage was the closure of the theatre altogether, followed by that depressing interval when the locked entrance would slowly fill up with waste paper until the day when some developer would come along and knock the whole place down. Really, it was the end of an era. It took time, mind you, more time than maybe I've suggested, but you could see the beginnings of it as the forties merged into the fifties.

The period was a transitional one for me, too, especially as some of the links formed unconsciously in wartime began to have their effect on my peacetime career. It was only now, for instance, that I came to realise that I was lucky enough to have a loyal and emotionally attached following in certain European countries, in particular the Scandinavian ones, and this set the pattern for my European movements for some years. It all came to light when I was invited to appear in Denmark on the strength of the enormous, illicit audience there that my wartime broadcasting had attracted. This was when I received the very humbling knowledge that they'd been risking their necks to hear me, and when I at last tumbled to the fact that the clear diction which people had always commented on was a real virtue. If the Danish audience was exceptionally large, it was probably because so many Danes spoke English. They also found that I was very easy to understand, so here, suddenly, I was presented with this hitherto unsuspected, ready-made audience. I was surprised, because until then I'd only ever thought of my wartime broadcasting in terms of an audience of British servicemen and the inhabitants of English-speaking countries. When I went to sing for the Danes, they had another surprise for me as well.

It was 1948 and the journey was my first peacetime flight. As we approached Copenhagen, the second pilot came back and said they had Danish radio on the radio telephone, wanting to speak to me. So I went forward into the cockpit and held a bit of a conversation and heard myself being welcomed to Denmark. Then the voice asked me if I'd say hello to the people; I muttered something, though it wasn't easy to listen or to speak or to concentrate with all the terrific crackle and noise going on.

When I'd finished speaking, I did manage to hear the voice at the other end say: 'Will you please sing to us?'

'Yes,' I said, 'but it's a bit difficult because I don't happen to have my piano with me at the moment, but I'll do my best.'

'Would you sing "Wish Me Luck?"'

I simply couldn't recall the words at all, so I did 'We'll Meet Again' as if I hadn't heard him. Then we said goodbye and that was that, or so I thought. We were met enthusiastically at the airport, driven to the Palace Hotel and conducted almost like royalty to our suite. There was a piano there, the room was all wired for sound and once again I was invited to say hello over Danish radio. The man from the Danish equivalent of *In Town Tonight* was there and we did a little interview. Once again there was a request for a song; once again it was for 'Wish Me Luck'. I couldn't believe it. Nor could I remember it, and my pianist, who was Barry Grey at that time, couldn't either. So I sang 'Yours'. At the end of it they all applauded politely, but said: 'You are going to do "Wish me Luck" at the concerts, aren't you?' Well, I could remember recording the song, but I had to own up to the promoter that I no longer knew it. 'But it is your signature tune over here, your biggest song,' he said, scandalized.

Well, it was all news to me; as far as I and everybody else in England was concerned, 'Wish Me Luck as You Wave Me Goodbye' was Gracie Fields' song, and I had merely made one of dozens of other versions of it. I suppose what had happened was that I'd done it on a broadcast, or the record had been heard over the air and just happened to catch my Danish listeners' fancy. I'd recorded it in November 1939, and presumably a few copies could have found their way to Denmark before the country was overrun by the Germans. Or perhaps Danish listeners had heard it on the occasional record programme from Britain and liked it enough for it to have become 'my' song there. But that didn't solve our immediate problem, and we still needed to get the music from somewhere.

Next day the promoter produced a piano copy, Barry hastily arranged it for the large orchestra that was to accompany me, Harry copied the parts, I brushed up on the words and the tune, and we got it into that night's concert. And a good job we did, because wherever we went where there was an orchestra or any live music, they would immediately strike up with 'Wish Me Luck'. I couldn't escape it.

One way and another the promoter must have thought we were an odd lot, for on top of my not knowing what he was convinced was my most successful record, I declined the invitation to do an extra concert. The group of five concerts had gone down so well, and he'd had to turn so many people away, that he wanted me to do an additional one; he guaranteed that it would be sold out. But I'd promised Virginia I'd be back on a certain day, and although at two years old she probably didn't know one day from another, I had made a promise, and that's all there was to it. The promoter, almost beside himself with disbelief, followed me to the airport begging me to stay. I think the only thing that convinced him I meant what I said was the sight of the aircraft taking off with me and Harry in it. We eventually went back again many times, but that was it for that first trip. It was on account of my attitude towards

Virginia, I might add, that I turned down an opportunity to go to Australia as early as 1947. We were offered sea trips each way for the three of us, but I thought it was too early in her life to uproot her for such a long time: it was to be sixteen years before we finally made the visit.

For a while, incidentally, our subsequent Continental journeys were by boat and train, for while Virginia was very small we thought flying too risky. I had never been too fond of aeroplanes ever since travelling to Burma, but the incident that put us off flying for a time came about on another occasion in Denmark. We were supposed to travel by air from there to Sweden, but the weather was so foul we couldn't go, and a concert had to be cancelled as a result. Not very long before, the American actress and soprano Grace Moore had been killed flying that very route in similar conditions. That was the last air trip that we allowed to be arranged for us for quite a time.

The easiest rail and sea journey of all was across to Holland. Very soon after the war I began visiting the Netherlands so often that for a while there were plenty of Dutch people who actually thought I lived there. I certainly felt at home there, enjoying a sense of kinship with the Dutch which grew steadily over the years. In fact it had begun even before the war. In the late thirties they heard me broadcasting with Ambrose (and Ambrose had a tremendous following there), and I also toured Holland with the band. So I was known to them before my wartime broadcasting took on any kind of special significance for them. The war hadn't been long over before Dutch radio got into the habit of inviting me to broadcast from Hilversum, and from that small beginning, by easy stages I became established in Holland as a concert artist. And when Dutch television was just getting started, I took part in a programme whose 'studio' was a curtained-off corner of a small converted church. As in Denmark, a pro-British attitude and the almost universal use of English as a second language were deciding factors in my success with the Dutch, and as record production got into its post-war stride, so my records did steadily better and better there. In fact concert promotion in Holland tended to be done rather more in collaboration with the record companies than it was here, and one of the people who was very energetic on my behalf in that field was Jerry Oord, who began in a modest way with a record shop and built up his business to the point where he got into the record-making side himself, with a company called Bovima. This he eventually sold to EMI, and he went on to become the managing director of EMI Records in London.

At the risk of getting ahead of my own story, it might be worth dwelling for a moment on my long love affair with the Dutch and their apparent affection for me. It's all intimately tied up with my ex-service connections, especially the benefit concerts held in Holland for the Escapers' Society. Through these I met Prince Bernhardt, a charming and affable man who invited me to all sorts of functions supported by the Dutch royal family. On one occasion I was asked to do the first concert in a brand-new entertainment complex called the Sportsdrome, at Beywerick, and also to be present at the opening ceremony earlier in the day. There we were with the royal party, on a tour of inspection, dutifully following His Royal

Highness in a long straggling snake round the building. Being a thorough man, he made sure that every door was opened, and having got as far as the splendidly appointed men's changing rooms, he proceeded to head through the entrance of what was obviously the loo. We trailed in behind him like children until he suddenly stopped and then began backing out rather hastily. In the confusion it was impossible to see what was going on, so I can only assume that one of the workmen had been christening the amenities in advance of the royal ceremony and been caught, so to speak, with his pants down.

Members of the Dutch royal family are very sociable and accessible, and I met Princess Marguerite at a Royal Air Force's Association ball in Holland (Princess Beatrix I met at the launching of a ship); and she suggested I drop in for tea sometime. It was a perfectly genuine invitation but I never did take her up on it.

The biggest single event – from a personal point of view – that I ever attended in Holland was a gigantic gala television concert in which I took part in 1962. There were recording artists from many countries there, each one doing something in the show; it was the sort of thing that tends to go on for ever, where you're lucky if you get on by midnight. Anyway, somebody had the bright idea of closing the programme with me, backed by a 100-strong choir, singing 'Land of Hope and Glory'. This is not so odd as it would appear, for the Dutch, apart from anything else, are very taken by that unique British institution, the Last Night of the Proms, which they hear over the radio or watch on television whenever they can. They are particularly impressed by the singing of patriotic songs, of which 'Land of Hope and Glory' is the best known and most stirring. So I hastily learned all the words of the seldom-sung verses (I needn't have bothered, as it turned out, because it was just the chorus that everybody wanted) and prepared to do it as a straightforward if unexpected closing number. But the response was like nothing I'd ever known before. At the end of it the audience went wild, and although it was television, they gave me a standing ovation there and then in the studio.

The pianist Russ Conway was there, running about saying, 'You've got to record this song,' and I must say I agreed with him. But I had a terrible time convincing Norman Newell, who was by then my recording manager, in spite of the telephone calls that started coming in from Holland requesting a record of the song. The inevitable happened and the Dutch Philips record people made a cover version of it, which did quite well. It was the future EMI MD Jerry Oord who said in the end: 'Look, you've got to do it,' and we eventually made it. In spite of the cover version, it got away, as they say in the trade, and earned me a Gold Disc. Even so, EMI, maybe feeling embarrassed that such an unfashionable song should have any appeal for the cynical, trendy sixties, refused to issue it in England.

As well as the Gold Disc for 'Land of Hope and Glory', I have another, less publicized but far more charming reminder of my long connection with Holland and the Dutch. They've stopped doing it now, but the Dutch airlines would sometimes give away to their regular passengers exquisite little pottery models of the beautiful eighteenth-century merchants' houses, with their handsome high gables, which line the Dutch city canals. I have a row of these, all different but all going together harmoniously, on a shelf in the big loft room of my present home in Sussex.

At the beginning of that post-war period there were still troop concerts to do, for the British Army of the Rhine was a huge force; one of my Continental tours was entirely for the British armed services in Germany. We saw devastated Essen on that trip, a timely reminder of what *we* had considered justifiable to do to *them*.

My activities were even slightly affected by what was going on – or not going on – in America. The boss of Decca, Mr E. R. Lewis as he was known then, was anxious to break into the American market and had started the London label there, on which he could issue things from the English Decca catalogue. But then in 1948 came one of those improbable episodes that happen from time to time in entertainment, and American recording musicians went on strike for a second time. Both this and the earlier recording ban, in 1944, had been over the increasing use in America of records for broadcasting, and once again the American Federation of Musicians simply downed instruments and refused to make any records. Mr Lewis took the opportunity to step up his campaign, including the making of some discs exclusively for America. 'Again' and 'You Can't Be True, Dear' were a couple that I did, and by the middle of 1948 'You Can't Be True, Dear' was doing very well, and in a sense preparing the ground for what was to come on the other side of the Atlantic.

CHAPTER TWELVE

Not My Style

B efore anything great could happen, there were to be disappointments, and the very end of the forties was rather a distressing time for me professionally. Not only were the variety theatres just starting to falter under the impact of television; there weren't all that number of good new songs about. But the worst thing, as far as I was concerned, had nothing to do with shifts of taste and the inevitable changes of fashion, but with one man's personal view of them. For in 1949 my hitherto regular work for the BBC – and I'd been broadcasting for a dozen years or more – suddenly stopped.

Harry and I had gone to see the then Head of Variety, ostensibly to discuss some future recording. But in fact, according to him, there wasn't to be any, because from the other side of his big desk in Aeolian Hall in London's New Bond Street he delivered his considered judgement that my kind of music was finished. He said that the 'sob stuff' wasn't wanted any more, and if I were to go on broadcasting I'd have to change my style.

There's not very much that makes me angry, but he couldn't have picked on a line of attack more calculated to make me furious than that. Leaving aside for a moment the matter of whether or not he knew what he was talking about, my style was me. Over the years I'd always stuck to my own particular brand of songs and my own particular way of singing them; I knew what suited me, and the public hadn't complained so far. While I wasn't against driving, rhythmic songs as such, I didn't see why I should have to switch over to completely different material – which wouldn't fit me – at the whim of a man who just happened to be responsible for the hiring and firing of entertainers. He was simply not interested in engaging me and, having rationalized his dislike, he added a final, patronizing insult: he had a programme he could put me into – somebody else's – in which I would be allowed to do 'one bright song'.

The interview didn't last long after that. As I say, I don't often get annoyed, but in effect I told him what he could do with his one bright number, and walked out.

It's a classic piece of self-delusion for an entertainer whose pride has been injured to say that he or she didn't need the work anyway but actually in my case it happened to be true, since, although I didn't know it, I was coming up to the busiest period of my whole life – even more than the wartime years. But what cut so deeply about this rejection by the BBC was that I had felt part of it, and it had been part of me. It was a crazy institution in many ways, but I loved it and it had helped to establish me. Through it I had been able to reach my truest public, been allowed to do something that had seemed really important. So while it was lovely to be making records and doing concerts and appearing on the variety stage, and while I could be occupied doing all these things, live broadcasting over the BBC was for me *the* link, the point of my most intimate contact with the people who – in spite of what one man so confidently insisted – I was sure still wanted to hear me. Apart from one rather grudging little series, not particularly well handled, in 1952, it would be almost seven years before I would be behind a BBC microphone with a programme of my own again.

From the point of view of work, though, in that period it was as if Fate had decided to devote itself to proving the Head of Variety wrong. I was so busy, and all my activities were so interconnected with each other, that it's very difficult to disentangle the threads. In case I should lose you on the way, what happened was that if the BBC didn't want to know, Radio Luxembourg certainly did, and what I did on one of their shows later contributed to the biggest hit record I'd ever had. In between times, however, I was in an enormously successful summer show at Blackpool, which eventually was transformed into a full-scale, long-running London stage production. Between Blackpool and London, I went to America for a series of appearances in Tallulah Bankhead's *Big Show* on radio. Out of Tallulah's shows came an offer (which I didn't take) of four years' work in America. And during the run of the London show I recorded that hit song I mentioned.

At Radio Luxembourg, a flourishing commercial station, they didn't seem to think my style was out of date, and I began recording programmes for them for the first time since before the war. They were regular and ran for a long time, and one particular series got a fair amount of publicity when, with

Radio Luxembourg's full approval, I was allowed to donate them, minus the commercial breaks, to the War Office for rebroadcasting to the British forces. My producer at Luxembourg was Frank Lee, who would later become A & R man at Decca and produced my records there, and one night he heard something that led eventually to a whole new style of backing a singer on record.

The programmes were originally to have been recorded in front of an invited audience in a London theatre. But Frank and I both felt that the best audience would be a 'service' one, and, as he knew the adjutant at RAF Uxbridge, he arranged for at least one of the programmes to be recorded there. I know we had Jack Jackson and Roberto Inglez with us, and it was very successful. One of the songs I did was 'The Last Mile Home', a wistful number on the obvious theme of the longest mile being the last mile home, and I was gratified when at one point the RAF boys joined in – not raucously, but really rather well. Frank, outside in the recording van, told me afterwards how the sound of seven hundred to a thousand airmen suddenly joining in hit him right in the stomach, how it seemed to him a bit of absolute magic. This we can use, sometime, somewhere, he thought to himself – and he would be proved right.

In the intervening time, however, I was caught up in a frantic whirl of professional activity. It began in Blackpool with a summer show in 1951. I was glad to be in it, for the shortage of good new songs of a style to suit me was becoming a problem, and I found I was recording a lot of old rope that didn't go anywhere. So when Leslie McDonnell was offered on my behalf the top of a bill which included Harry Secombe and the Bernard Brothers, with special production numbers in it for me, I jumped at it. We rented a house up there, and the show ran for a wonderful sixteen weeks – a long time for an English summer resort. The Bernard Brothers had a hilarious act in those days, which included the two of them appearing in gingham dresses, with enormous bows in their hair, and miming to Andrews Sisters' records. Harry Secombe was practically unknown, and still doing the comic shaving act that he started with at the Windmill. He was chubby, of course, even then, and – unlike a lot of comics – exactly the same likeable clown off the stage as he was on. It was such an attractive, warm, successful production that the bandleader and impresario Jack Hylton became anxious to base a London show on it.

Naturally it takes quite a while to re-jig an entire presentation for the West End and to find a suitable theatre for it, but I had so much to occupy me that I could actually have done with more time between shows rather than less. For, while they were preparing the production that would emerge as *London Laughs*, I was away in America doing a regular guest spot on Tallulah Bankhead's radio programme – a lavish and prestigious affair called *The Big Show*. Tallulah was an extreme Anglophile; I don't think that had made her uncritical of us, but she truly loved anything British, and she was in England in the late summer of 1951 to do a kind of London edition of her programme. Apparently she was having lunch with Ambrose somewhere in London one day and, as Ambrose tells it, she heard my voice coming over the radio or on a record or from somewhere, and decided she wanted me for her show.

I didn't learn this until some years later, so at the time Tallulah appeared to have picked me out of the blue. The first I heard of it was a telephone call from Leslie McDonnell while I was still in the Blackpool show. At that period the one thing I longed to do, for some reason, was play principal boy in an English pantomime, and when he said, obviously excited, 'Guess what I've managed to get for you,' I immediately came back with, 'A pantomime!' 'No,' he said, 'better than that.' Well, as far as I was concerned, there wasn't anything better than that, and when he told me it was a radio show, to be recorded at the Palladium for the United States, I'm afraid I was a lot less enthusiastic than I ought to have been. I just couldn't have guessed what it would lead to.

Tallulah, an extravagantly showbiz kind of person, at least twice as large as life, was outwardly one of those strong professional 'personalities' from whom, since I'm diffident by nature, I would normally run a mile away. But she was kind and wonderful and a complete joy to be with. She took to me, she took to my voice and she made everything so easy that before I knew it I'd embarked on what turned out to be several very happy months. At first it was just the recording at the London Palladium – and what a cast: the *All About Eve* actor George Sanders, Jack Buchanan (who later starred in *The Band Wagon* opposite Fred Astaire), comic actress Beatrice Lillie, Meredith Willson (later he would write *The Music Man*), all presided over by the magnificent Tallulah. It will give you an idea of the friendly atmosphere of the show when I say that on my souvenir programme Meredith Willson wrote 'Vera is loved', because I sang 'I Am Loved'.

The outcome of all this was that I was then asked to go to New York and appear in four more programmes with Tallulah. Virginia was now four and a half, and after a spot of debate with ourselves we decided that we could go, and that we could leave her behind for a while. Soon, she would be starting school, and it would then be too late, for I think that once a child begins its school career it needs a stable home life. So we went. We were away longer than we anticipated, for the four weeks were quickly extended to eight. In the event, I did seven, because Jack Hylton brought forward by one week the Oxford try-out of his now completely remodelled *London Laughs* and I had to dash back for that.

We had a great time in New York. Tallulah insisted that I do two songs in each show, which seemed to suit everybody, except one of her guests one week. For some reason Betty Hutton (the star of *Annie Get Your Gun*) took exception to what she appeared to think was the 'teacher's pet' status of this, to her, unknown English singer, and was vastly put out that I should be doing two numbers to her one. So put out, in fact, that she sulked publicly all the way through it. *The Big Show* was conducted rather along the lines that became accepted for TV chat shows, in that all the guests were in full view of the studio audience all the time. So, except when she was actually performing at the microphone, Betty Hutton sat elaborately with her back to me throughout the entire programme. To do so she must have made herself quite uncomfortable physically, while it clearly made the audience uncomfortable in another sense because it was so embarrassingly childish. I don't know whether she said anything afterwards, but Tallulah blithely ignored it, making it quite plain that I was doing my two songs and that was that.

A very young Tony Bennett, then just getting started, was in *The Big Show*, but he, on the other hand, couldn't have been more pleasant or modest. He would clock up his first million-seller some time in 1952 with 'Because of You', but anyone with less of that 'star' attitude would be hard to imagine.

Perhaps because the atmosphere and circumstances were different, and because for almost three months we didn't have our permanent home to go to but just an apartment, our social life was much more active in New York than in England. Practically every night after the broadcast we'd go to Lindy's, *the* hangout for show people and a great place for food, right at Times Square and Broadway. It was there, in fact, that I committed a great tactical error as far as food is concerned. Some time towards three in the morning, Harry would regularly make a pig of himself on Lindy's strawberry cheesecake. For nearly three months I refused to try it, on the grounds that I didn't like cheese. On the night before we were due to sail home Harry coaxed me into tasting a bit of his. It was out of this world; it was so fantastic. I was furious – for three months I'd been denying myself this treat! Because of course it didn't taste cheesy at all. For some time after that somebody used to send me one of these things over every week by air. That's how good it was.

My last night in the show was very moving. Tallulah said how sorry she was that I'd got to go back to England and then she got the whole audience – two or three thousand people – up on their feet and, with alternate rows swaying in opposite directions, they sang 'Auld Lang Syne'. It was one of those real lump-in-throat moments and I felt proud and sad at the same time.

But I had *London Laughs* to look forward to. It had become very changed from its original Blackpool prototype, with a radically different cast. Jimmy Edwards, then approaching the peak of his radio career in *Take It From Here*, which had been running on and off for about three years, was one of the two comedians. The other was to have been Jimmy's colleague in *Take It From Here*, Dick Bentley, but I gather there'd been some disagreement over billing and Dick had dropped out. So in came Tony Hancock, the latest name to be established by that star-making radio series *Educating Archie*.

People always want to know what the other members of a cast were like, but the fact is that a group of people working in a show tend to see very little of each other outside it. You come to the theatre, you go to your dressing room, you dress and do your make-up. Then you go on stage, either with or without the rest of the cast, you do your stuff and you come off. While you're waiting about for the next call, your colleagues are working, doing *their* part of the show. When it's all over, you're all very tired – maybe some people in the cast even have to hurry off to do a late-night cabaret spot some-where; but whatever the case, it's usual for everybody to go their separate ways.

Even in those circumstances, however, it was obvious that Tony Hancock was a genius, and that he was also a troubled one. Every night, as I waited to go on, I would hear him work-ing, listen to him polishing, perfecting his act, hear him trying to extract from the audience the vast quantities of laughter his appetite needed. In those days he was driving himself ruthlessly towards the edge of the precipice, and twice he reached that awful state of nerves which made him blurt out, 'I can't go on; I can't go on,' and mean it literally. He would be off for a few weeks then, getting his health and confidence back – and this was before he'd reached the real big time. Apart from that, he kept himself to himself, and would have been hard to get to know even if there had been time.

Some people have claimed that Jimmy Edwards was difficult to get on with. Well, maybe, but to me he was just marvellous, invariably good-humoured and as kind as anyone I've worked with. We used to do a spot in the show together, which he would vary each night, according to how he felt, and it was pure pleasure to work with him. I would call him 'Jim Jam', which was a liberty I'd take with very few colleagues.

Jim derived huge amusement from the fact that I occupied my free time during the show running things up on a hand sewing machine in a little room that led off my dressing room. The moment I came off I'd slip out of my dress, put on my old dressing gown and start cranking away for dear life, for the one thing I can't stand is that awful feeling of wasting time during those long gaps when you're not wanted on stage. I'd made clothes for Virginia on a hand machine at Blackpool, and at the Adelphi I made practically all the curtains and cushion covers for Three Beams, in Ditchling. I made lampshades, too, and the chorus girls were so intrigued that I was soon running something like a class in lampshade making, with half the chorus in attendance.

Although I loved performing, I was often thinking about home and my duties as a wife and mother. There was one particular night when, during a scene we did together, Jimmy noticed me involuntarily putting my hand to my forehead. When we came off he said, all solicitously: 'What's wrong? Is your migraine troubling you – I saw you go to hold your head.' And I just had to own up that at that moment I'd suddenly remembered I hadn't turned the gas out under the ham I'd been boiling at home!

London Laughs opened at the Adelphi, in the Strand, in April 1952, and settled down for what promised to be a satisfactory run. It was, incidentally, probably the last major show of its kind to rely heavily for its appeal on radio names rather than those from television. In view of the situation between me and the BBC, perhaps it's not quite accurate to include me as a radio name so much as one from the world of records. What is certain is that by the time the show was four months old I was very firmly part of the recording scene, having just had the biggest hit of my entire career. And as a tune, this song had the strangest history of any of them.

The story of it began in 1950, in Lucerne, where Harry and I had gone for a short holiday. Over the hotel radio one day we heard a record of some young children singing. We couldn't assess its possibilities as a song, for it was in German, but we liked the tune, one of those easily memorized, insistent, old-fashioned kind of melodies that eventually you can't get out of your head. Then one evening we went to a beer garden, and a great buxom girl got up on the stage and sang the same song, and everybody joined in, swaying from side to side and waving their beer mugs. It revolved mainly round the words *auf wiederseh'n*, which is the exact equivalent of the French *au revoir* – 'till we meet again'. I said to Harry: 'There's that song again, and it's a hit if there ever was one.' When we got home, we tried to trace it, but nobody seemed to know who published it, not even the publisher who had it in his catalogue at the time which was Peter Maurice, where all our old friends like Wally Ridley were, and where we'd gone first in our search.

Anyhow, nearly two years went by and then Bunny Lewis of Decca brought us a batch of tunes. I listened to one of them and said: 'This is the tune we've been going mad looking for.' 'There's no lyric yet.' 'Never mind, let's get on to Frank Lee.' Frank was producing my records at Decca by now, and I told him: 'It's got no lyric yet, but here's the song we're going to do with the servicemen.' He agreed right away, and of course that's how 'Auf Wiederseh'n, Sweetheart' was done, only in a studio, and with the soldiers', airmen's and sailors' chorus drawn from all three services. The tune and the original German words had been written about three years earlier by Eberhard Storch, and new English words were supplied by Geoffrey Parsons and Jimmy Phillips. As Frank Lee and I and Roland Shaw, the musical director, did it in the first place, it had an extra verse in it, but Mr E.R. Lewis, of Decca, said it was too long like that and had the verse cut out. He was in the middle of one of his vigorous campaigns to establish English records in America at the time, and I shall always remember two other things he said about it. First, that it was to be cut 'good and deep and loud' on the final disc so as to be heard over car radios in traffic jams in New York; and secondly –

having sent thousands of copies to America (I think he flew them over) – the instruction he wanted passed on to his transatlantic sales staff was: 'Tell them either to sell them or eat them.'

They sold them to such good effect that it became the first ever British record to top the hit parade simultaneously on both sides of the Atlantic. As a matter of fact, I was the first British popular singer to make it all the way to the top of those great long charts they publish in trade magazines like *Variety* and *Billboard*. I don't know how they work them all out, because there are about a hundred titles on them, but it was very gratifying. 'Auf Wiederseh'n, Sweetheart' was a huge hit here, too, of course, and its success slopped over to affect *London Laughs*, for it broke right in the middle of the summer, when London stage shows are often struggling with fine weather and people's general reluctance to go to the theatre in the long light evenings. The show was passing through just such a period, but 'Auf Wiederseh'n' brought them back in again.

After that, *London Laughs* just kept running, which was both a pleasure and a bore, because while it's good for your morale to be in a successful show, it's bad for your artistic muscles to go on doing the same routine night after night. I didn't experience the thing that sometimes happens to actors in long runs, where they suddenly find themselves halfway through Act Two without having the faintest idea how they got there. I think what happened to me was worse. I had one or two lovely production numbers in it, including one for which I wore a marvellous, extravagant, turquoise dress in three tiers with voluminous pleats and a huge, picture hat, and sat in an open four-wheel carriage drawn by a pair of mechanical horses; that was for a song called 'It's Wonderful to Be in Love'. Another, the opening, was set in an elaborate Covent Garden market scene, and it was in this one that one night I simply forgot the words. Often when that happens the opening bars of music are enough to get you going, but since this was a number specially written for the show, with none of the instant familiarity that goes with a standard song, it didn't work like that. My mind was a complete blank; what came out of my mouth eventually I don't know, but I just had to try to write a song on the spot. I worked through all the flowers and vegetables I could find rhymes for, and rhubarbed my way through. Before the next show, I had to learn the song all over again.

Still, that's a problem that goes with a success, not a flop. Yet the BBC's Head of Variety wasn't interested. He actually had the gall to allow himself to be quoted in the press to the effect that he was looking for 'another Vera Lynn', while the original one was readily available little more than a mile away in the Strand. I suppose the most ironic touch of all was when the situation reached the point as described in a cutting dating from November 1953:

BBC STILL BEING DIFFICULT

Vera Lynn braved a bad cold to face the microphone last weekend recording a programme to be broadcast on Christmas Day – but you're not going to hear it. 'Vera's Christmas Song' was requested by the BBC's American branch in New York and they plan to sell it to a commercial broadcasting company for relay coast-to-coast on Christmas Day.

The domestic BBC's reason for not transmitting it themselves was: 'It does not fit in with our schedules.'

So there I was, towards Christmas 1953, using all the BBC's facilities to make a programme on the strength, apparently, of popular demand across the Atlantic, while being denied those facilities to broadcast to my fellow countrymen. There had just been the one brief series of 'Let's Meet Again' in mid-1952, with the comedians Tony Fayne and David Evans, and after that, once again, nothing. And that can't have amounted to much, either, since I had almost completely forgotten about it.

But throughout it all, as ever, I had the press on my side, and I must say they were wonderful to me, never losing an opportunity to get a word in on my behalf. But as I said, though it would have been satisfying to have been back, I didn't actually need to be broadcasting for the BBC. *London Laughs* was still doing tremendous business when it finally had to come off in February 1954. It could have run longer, but for the fact that Jimmy Edwards and I, never having foreseen such a success for the show, had contracts to go and do other things.

These were to take me first back to America, then into commercial television, and finally – would you believe it? – home again to the BBC.

CHAPTER THIRTEEN

Round & About

When I was in America doing Tallulah Bankhead's *Big Show*, the producers paid me the compliment of telling me that I sang with an English accent but phrased a lyric like an American singer. I can only suppose they thought that all English singers were of the Jessie Matthews-musical comedy school, which is an immediately recognizable and uniquely British style. Anyway, I took it to imply that I stood a good chance of being accepted if I ever decided to make the break and settle there. And it could have come to that. After the Tallulah series, NBC, whose network it went out on, offered me an enormously lucrative four-year contract, while Tutti Camarata, the brilliant arranger and conductor, wanted me to go and work for the Disney studios. These were tempting offers, but they meant leaving England, if not for good, then for a long time, and I didn't want to do that. And as well as being patriotic, feeling that I belonged here, I was always very family conscious; although we didn't live in each other's pockets, we were a close family emotionally, and didn't like our being too scattered physically.

So long as I could find enough work in my own country I was happy to do that; the chance of international acclaim wasn't that important to me, and I would rather stay in England, at ease with myself and among the people I needed, than go slogging away after some apparently bigger prize. But an offer to go back for a strictly limited period was something I could accept – indeed, should accept. After all, although nearly two years had gone by since 'Auf Wiederseh'n', which is a long time in popular music, I had had a number one in America, and it probably still counted for something. Besides, I might never do that again, and it would be a pity to lose that little advantage.

So I went to Las Vegas with a show booked to run four weeks and purporting to typify London. Unfortunately, it just didn't work. For a start, its American producer had never been to England, and he seemed to have got all his notions about London from old Hollywood B pictures, out-of-date guide-books and his own inaccurate guesswork. You can imagine what it was like. He even had the chorus girls walking across the stage with the artists' names on placards, as they once did in very old-fashioned shows. Secondly, Las Vegas was clearly not ready for Tommy Cooper, who was devastatingly funny in the show, as always, but simply too original and unusual for an average American audience. So this ill-conceived extravaganza slithered to a halt after a fortnight, though it wasn't the total disaster it might have been, for the tough gambling bosses who were footing the bill were persuaded that it wasn't the English cast's fault, and everybody got paid in full. Vegas is no place to be stranded in without money. I loved it out there, though. I thought it was so exciting. It was unlike anything I had ever seen before. Of course, it's completely different now: it was just one strip when I was there, with all the clubs down one road.

Those gambling bosses, who ran everything out there, really were incredible characters; it was almost as if they were trying to live up to Hollywood versions of themselves. They were hard nuts, but always with those redeeming soft spots. They treated me like Dresden china, they called me 'The Queen' and they wouldn't let me go near the gaming tables. One night I strolled into the casino and merely said, 'How do you play this?' It was pure curiosity, but I'd hardly taken half a dozen steps before one of them steered me away. 'Not you,' he said, 'not you. You're not leaving your salary behind.' But the tough side ultimately ruled their lives, and it was only a few years later that we heard that one of them we had known, the charming and ebullient Gus Greenbaum, had been battered to death in a grisly, unsolved murder in which his wife, Bess, was also killed. I believe it finally went down in police records as a 'revenge killing', though revenge for what nobody ventured to say.

If the failure of the show was a disappointment, the trip itself was enormous fun. On the way there we had stopped in New York long enough for me to appear in a television production called *The Show of Shows* with Sid Caesar and Imogene Coca. When it was over, most of the cast escorted Harry and me to the station and saw us aboard the Santa Fe *Chief* with such a wealth of flowers and fuss and kissing and hugging and 'good-lucking' that our steward immediately assumed we were newly-weds, and fluttered around us with every imaginable attention for the next two and a half days.

He was so wonderful to us that we didn't try to undeceive him, and acted our parts all the way. After thirteen years of married life, that wasn't bad. Although a lot of it was across flat country and even desert, I loved the long train journey, with its observation car, its wonderful food and the two berths opening into one to form a sort of lounge.

Our arrival in Las Vegas somehow set the tone for the show itself, for there was no one to meet us, and eventually we made our way to the Flamingo by cab. And there we encountered that strange combination of instant hostility and equally instant friendliness which seems to be a characteristic of American life. For when we went to check in, the man at the desk, hardly bothering to look up, said, 'Name?'

We told him.

'Nothing here,' he said, and that appeared to conclude the conversation.

'But we're booked in here,' said Harry, 'Vera Lynn's appearing here.'

'Don't know anything about it.'

'We'd better talk to the manager.'

'Waste of time. I tell you we got nothing about you coming here.'

It didn't seem to matter that my name was in big letters on the outside of the building, but eventually we did get the manager, or someone, and, with the same lack of interest that had been going on through the whole thing, he just said: 'OK. Give 'em a room.' Once we'd got in the place, though, as I said earlier, they gave us a great time. It was almost as if they were trying to test you, to see what you'd take.

After the show folded, Harry and I decided to make a virtue of necessity and stay on for a week to see some of the other productions Las Vegas had to offer, and generally relax. That's how we came to be in the Last Frontier one night when Tommy Dorsey's band was playing. As soon as he spotted us he took the band into a number from the old Ambrose days (that'll give you an idea of Ammy's standing among bandleaders, incidentally) and afterwards he came over and joined us and chatted. He had a reputation for having a fiery temper, but he couldn't have been more affable and charming. And what a musician; they say that Frank Sinatra learned his extraordinary breath control simply from watching Tommy Dorsey play the trombone night after night while Sinatra was Dorsey's male singer in the early forties, and I can well believe it. He played one of his big hits, 'Song of India', while we were there, and he hardly seemed to need to breathe at all.

It's odd how differently people behave. Tommy Dorsey went out of his way to greet us and make us feel welcome. But when we visited Hollywood, and had lunch in one of the big studio canteens, an opposite sort of situation developed. Michael Wilding, who was then married to Elizabeth Taylor, saw us and came over, as he put it, 'for a breath of England', and stayed talking for a long time. Elizabeth Taylor, on the other hand, never even looked in our direction. We were in Hollywood because we were also visiting Los Angeles to look up Joe Pasternak, the film director who had more or less discovered Deanna Durbin nearly twenty years earlier, and who had more recently brought the turbulent Mario Lanza to fame on the screen. Joe, whose spoken English was still difficult to follow even after twenty years in California, had written a song that I had done, called 'Little Home'.

There were, of course, constant visits to Scandinavia, visits so frequent that, like the wartime hospital and troop concerts, and all those places in Burma, it is difficult to distinguish one from another in retrospect. One little incident I always connect with Odense, the birthplace of Hans Christian Andersen. The little town and its facilities weren't geared to the huge numbers of people who came pouring in for the concert. The one sizeable hotel, where we were staying, was crammed to the doors, and its restaurant ran out of more or less everything in turn – room, waiters, cutlery and, finally, food. We'd worked hard and we were all starving, but there was nothing for it but to wait. To while away the time, Harry, Barry Grey and Rawicz and Landauer, those uncanny piano duettists, consoled themselves drinking schnapps with lager chasers. After about an hour and a half of this self-inflicted injury, they got up and went unsteadily to the loo, singing 'Why are we waiting?' in a selection of keys as they threaded their way through the crowd. 'These drunken English,' somebody said as they went by, which seemed a bit unfair, since it was because of us that all these people were there in the first place, and here we were, the only ones not getting served. I think the drunken English on that occasion behaved with great restraint.

Another time wasn't funny at all. This was in 1954, in Gothenburg. It was just before the last concert of a tour, and the telephone rang in our hotel room. As anybody who's ever tried to call me has found out, it's always Harry who answers, but on this one occasion Harry was in the shower, so I picked it up. It was the text of a telegram telling me my father was dead.

It was not quite the shock it might have been. He had been confined to his bed when the trip had started, and he'd been ill on and off for the previous six or seven years. After having pneumonia at the age of seventeen, he'd got through the rest of his life on one lung, including a period as a glass-blower, though God knows how he'd managed that. The net result was that he'd always been prone to chest ailments, and his dying had been a possibility never far from our minds during the last few years.

I went on that night because what else could I have done? We were due to leave the next morning anyway, so nothing would be achieved by dashing home a few hours sooner to a situation already out of anyone's control. From the public's point of view, money had been paid and tickets sold. What purpose would have been served by letting all those people down? Besides, cancelling the concert was not a gesture that my father would have appreciated. It was a sad homecoming, though, for Harry as well as for me, since Harry and my dad had been pals right from the beginning. Harry loathed pubs, but whenever he was in Barking my dad always insisted on taking him up to his local, the Royal Oak, to see Jock the Potman, a local character who worked in the pub, and have a chat with his mates. And Harry would always go, because he loved my dad much more than he hated pubs.

I think everybody who knew him was fond of Dad; he was companionable without being aggressively hearty, he loved his home and his family and his friends and his club. He was easy going and took everything just as it came, from Ladysmith Avenue to Clayton Holt. He was proud of me and he encouraged me in his own quiet way, but if what I'd wanted when I left school had been to stay in that place sewing on buttons, that would have been all right with him. 'Do what you want to, mate,' he'd say. I only hope he knew how much I appreciated him.

I've no idea what sort of show I gave that night. Once you've been doing it long enough there's a level of professional competence which I don't think you fall below – unless you're physically ill, that is – and in any case I doubt if the news had managed to sink in and take effect by the time I went on. Going on at all in these circumstances might sound like callousness, but where there's nothing practical you can do it's probably better for the artist to work than not to work. It would have been part of Dad's own philosophy to go along with that.

In the larger world of popular music generally, rock'n'roll and skiffle were coming, but they had far less effect on my life than I would have expected. The real changes were to come in the early sixties. During the mid-fifties I was still getting offers of shows along the lines of *London Laughs* but, successful though that had been, I decided against them. The very popularity of *London Laughs* had created its own problems, the worst of which was the way it cut across my intention of being a proper mother. As soon as Virginia started school we had the crazy situation that just as she was coming home in the afternoon, I was getting ready for work. It was like shifts changing over in a factory. I just wasn't prepared to face the possibility of another long run. Luckily for me, the answer was to be television.

Harry, meanwhile, was to be rather less fortunate in his next venture, even though it involved me in a marginal tangle with skiffle myself. Harry still always came with me wherever I was working, to act as watchdog over the all-important sound and lighting systems, but that left him with a certain amount of time and energy to spare. So in the early fifties he went into music publishing as well. It wasn't the best time in history to do it, because the day when the performer was to be his own composer and his own publisher was rapidly approaching, but it was still possible to pick up a potential hit in the then-accepted way of somebody bringing you a song, and you finding an artist for it and persuading a record company to record it. For Harry the big number was to be an old, traditional tune, apparently long out of copyright, with a new lyric by Jack Fishman, called 'Travelling Home'. I sang it straight, over a kind of busy, skiffle sort of rhythm, and the thing immediately took off in America, selling 75,000 there within a few days of release. Unfortunately, another publisher claimed the copyright and got an injunction put on it, so that no more copies could be pressed and sold. Although we won our case in the end, it took about eighteen months to bring it to court, by which time the song was dead beyond any hope of reviving. A pity, because the case itself was made memorable and spectacular by the fact that we called as witnesses a number of enormous, colourful Scots pipe majors who substantiated our claim that the tune had been played as a traditional air for as long as any piper could remember. It was an even greater pity from the point of view of Harry's publishing venture, because that one hit would have set it on it feet; as it was, it never had a real chance. Later on Harry went into the publishing side of EMI for a while.

It was television and radio that kept me busy for the second half of the fifties. Talk about the longest mile being the last mile home – it couldn't have been much longer than the roundabout route I followed back to the BBC. It was the coming of Independent Television in 1955 that did it, for they hadn't been going very long before they gave me a series which ran for seventeen weeks, and was mildly successful in spite of behind-the-scenes problems. For the people watching at home some of the shows must have looked very strange. Everything was done live then, and this particular director's rehearsal technique was so chaotic and lopsided that for the first week the final fifteen minutes of the show were done without any kind of camera or lighting rehearsal whatever, and only the sketchiest of preparation of any sort. So there was the first part of the programme all crisply presented, followed by a tail end in which everybody was busking furiously to stave off disaster. That's fine in an occasional emergency, and you should be prepared to do it once in a while, but in a proper, regular show I did like to know what was going on. Every week there was some kind of chaos and it got so bad that the studio hands and the technicians began taking bets on how much longer I'd stand it. '*This* week she *must* blow her top,' they'd predict, as they adjusted the odds.

Meanwhile, Harry was having his own troubles up in the producer's gallery, the equivalent of the control cubicle in a sound studio. Or rather, outside it, for having kept up his usual barrage of complaints, all justified, about the sound, one night he was told to leave the box by the producer, and forbidden to set foot in it again. So Harry left. Next morning, though, Jack Hylton was on the telephone to him. 'What the hell was wrong with the sound last night, Harry?' So Harry had to tell him that the producer wouldn't let him in the gallery. Hylton called a meeting – himself, Leslie McDonnell, the songwriter Hughie Charles, Harry, me, one or two others and the producer. Unfortunately, the producer never got to put his side of it at all. He turned up an hour late, and Jack Hylton, when he was told he'd finally arrived, said, 'Tell him not to bother,' and he was out. Commercial television was pretty ruthless; mind you, it came out later that this particular man claimed to be tone deaf, which probably explained a good deal.

One very pleasant factor about these otherwise turbulent shows was that – since these were the days when artists themselves hadn't started doing their own presentation – I was able to use a very young and handsome David Jacobs as my compère.

In 1956, the year – for us in Britain – of rock'n'roll, cinema-seat-ripping, Bill Haley, Elvis Presley and Tommy Steele, there was, surprisingly enough, still room for me. Within the space of a few weeks I began both radio and television shows for the BBC, the fruits of an exclusive two-year contract with the corporation. It was an unprecedented offer allowing me TV shows, radio shows and a separate series of record programmes with me as disc jockey. I was back, and it meant a lot to me.

In practical terms one of the things being back at the BBC meant was the start of an association with television producer Albert Stevenson, which was to result in over seventy programmes. These began in October 1956, and usually went out fortnightly in groups of twelve, so that one series would cover twenty-four weeks, with the alternative Monday night (or whatever) occupied by something like the Billy Cotton show. Albert was lovely. He was a real pro, who'd come up through jobs like stage managing at the Shepherd's Bush Empire, and who knew what was what. Most importantly, he saw eye to eye with Harry, and instead of throwing his weight about and ordering Harry out of the box and all that nonsense, he encouraged Harry to work with him. The result was that I was happy, the atmosphere of the programmes was happy and they were as good, technically, as they could have been at that date. And Albert was always willing to try things. Studio equipment was nothing like as flexible and adaptable as it is today, and there were still a lot of restrictions on how much the artist could move about the set. But I was especially keen to do a finale in one edition which would let me go to each of the artists taking part in turn and thank them that way, instead of having each one arrive, one after another, on some fixed spot. Albert wasn't sure if he'd be able to follow me, but he was good enough to try, and because he and his crews were marvellous at their jobs, it worked.

I was allowed to present these shows myself, and that led to another pleasant little convention. Albert needed time at one point to get everything just right for one fairly elaborate scene each week – a ballet or something like that – and the pleasant device we evolved for getting those few minutes' breathing space was a little ad-lib chat between Eric Robinson and me. One week I broke off the conversation and said: 'I suppose you know why we have this little talk here every week, don't you, Eric?' All innocence, he said he didn't. 'Well, it's just to give the studio time to get the next scene ready.' It was the simple truth, but he wasn't prepared for it, and he fell about – followed soon by me and everybody else. Just a tiny incident, but it was the sort of casual relaxation we tried to get into the show, and the kind of thing you could now do on television; it was starting to loosen up. You were no longer ruled by the chalk-mark on the floor and the stilted, laboriously learned script. Albert imposed one rigid rule on himself. As the sixties wore on, the scene became more and more dominated by the groups, and it became the trendy thing to let them loose in all kinds of TV shows, but he wouldn't hear of mixing the styles and the generations in my series.

While the series was running, Albert Stevenson came with me on my third trip to New York. This wasn't a working visit in the ordinary sense, for we were going as observers, the idea being that we should watch American television techniques at first hand. We went in particular to get behind the scenes of the *Perry Como Show*. As far as Albert and I were concerned, the secret of the programme's success was Perry Como himself, not the technicalities behind him. While I don't want to knock American television, which was neatly geared to American audiences, with respect I must say that I didn't feel they could teach us much technically.

In fact the only thing that ever bothered me was the increasing difficulty of finding new songs of a kind I wanted to sing and could sound true to myself in. This shortage of material – for they really didn't seem to be writing songs like they used to – was, as I recollect, the underlying reason for the long sequence of television shows coming to an end. Problems with songs were also connected with my leaving Decca in 1960, after nearly twenty-five years. There had been awkward moments in the mid-fifties, like the occasion when they tried to persuade me I ought to do 'A House with Love in It' with a Four Aces sound – you remember that undulating, 'scooping' way they attacked words? I said no, because my fans would wonder what I was trying to prove, and I think in the end we settled for some kind of compromise, with a touch of what they wanted in the backing. It was a straw in the wind, I suppose, and as the sixties began the song drought, as far as I was concerned, was becoming acute. So I began to think the time had come to make a move, and when my contract came up for renewal, I didn't take up the option, and went instead to EMI. I didn't really want to go, but the people, the times and the music had changed.

*   *   *

My family circumstances changed too. Virginia was now sixteen and ready to leave school; we knew she wasn't going to sing or dance or entertain, so the plan was to let her go to secretarial college for a year. But there was nothing to stop her coming on an extended trip with us before that. Offers for a tour of Australia and New Zealand, first made back in 1947, were still coming in. So, with the cupboard just about bare as far as suitable new songs were concerned, with no television series in sight, the variety theatre as good as dead and rock music apparently drowning everything else with its sheer volume, this seemed the moment to say, right, we're off.

Accordingly, our first visit to Australia was arranged for 1963. We gave Virginia the choice of going to Switzerland or having a different sort of education by travelling round the world with us and she decided, without any hesitation, that she'd rather come with us. Once again we were a compact family unit, only this time Virginia was practically grown up.

Merely preparing to go to Australia was exciting. More than for most trips I needed a whole new wardrobe, because I knew this was liable to be as much a social affair as a working, professional one, and that apart from singing I was going to have a busy time simply meeting people. Ex-service organizations had planned to throw luncheon parties all over the place, and I could expect to spend more time chatting than in actual performance. In fact, apart from wartime Burma, I've never been anywhere where more people wanted to meet me and talk to me than in Australia and New Zealand, and I don't think I've ever done so many interviews.

I had expected to meet nostalgic ex-servicemen with their wonderful gift of remembering the companionship and forgetting the grimness of wartime, but I was surprised and flattered at the number of entire families who wanted to come and talk to me. Many of them had emigrated to Australia or New Zealand soon after the war, and as they saw it, I was taking a part of their old home out to them. And they would always bring their children in an attempt to show them what the link meant to them. Native Australians also still had, at that time, that emotional tie with us which allowed them to think of England as home, even if they'd never been there. To them, too, I was a representative of the old country. And the public reception I got was more than I could ever have imagined. At one point on the tour there was a whole motorcade to escort me into town from the airport, and, as we got nearer the centre, throngs of parents and children lining the route. It was unbelievable. You wonder what on earth you can possibly do to live up to it.

Not that there was a lot of time to wonder about anything very much. Starting with dates in New Zealand, I did forty-eight concerts in forty days. Perth, Sydney, Brisbane – once more the names began to go by in a blur, for there was never any chance to see the places so that they could register as individual cities. Nor could I enjoy any of those natural assets that Australia and New Zealand have to offer – the sun and the swimming. A tour is work, work is singing, and the sun plays havoc with the voice – my voice anyway – while swimming leaves you open to all those infections which go straight to the throat and larynx. Don't let any promoter tell you that there's such a thing as a working holiday for an entertainer. Apart from needing to keep yourself in a fairly taut condition to give of your best, when you're on holiday there's a tendency to take risks – of getting colds and sore throats or tiring yourself out – which don't matter when you're there purely for fun and are answerable only to yourself, but which can be disastrous when thousands of people are counting on you.

But whatever precautions you take against external things, there's nothing much you can do about your own fatigue, and near the end of the tour, in Sydney, I collapsed in a state of nervous exhaustion. We had to cancel a concert and stick it on to the very end of the visit. It's a terrible feeling to realize that you simply cannot call on another ounce of energy from anywhere, that everything has been drained out of you and that you just have to stop, like machinery that won't work. Even more astounding, though, is a human being's capacity for recovery after a short rest.

Except for that one incident, the Australian experience was marvellous. Virginia had her seventeenth birthday in Sydney, complete with an immense cake. In fact, she had two birthdays in one day, because we were flying from Sydney to another engagement, and left Sydney after one celebration only to arrive in time for another.

Musically we had no problems, for we travelled with Eddie Calvert and the small band he had, and his pianist, Red Nichols, acted as my musical director for the trip. Eddie had had an enormous hit ten years previously with 'O Mein Papa' and, naturally enough, he was still expected to play it. It's interesting that both of us should have got our biggest records from German originals, and that Eddie Calvert's should have had a similar history to that of 'Auf Wiederseh'n', for I believe that 'O Mein Papa' first came to the notice of Norrie Paramor, who was producing Eddie's records for Columbia, through Norrie's au pair girl, who was able to identify a tune which either Eddie or Norrie had heard on the Continent. And when the vocal versions followed Eddie's hit instrumental, the English words, like those of 'Auf Wiederseh'n', were by Jimmy Phillips and Geoffrey Parsons.

Anyway, there I was with a ready-made group to back me, and therefore no problems over constantly having to rehearse with different musicians. We never carried our own public address system either. If Harry could get the co-operation of the sound man in a theatre, and had enough time to go over our requirements with him, he could usually get the existing system to suit me. This was where Harry was indispensable: he knew the effect we were aiming at, and he had the ability to charm, cajole or bully – according to necessity – whoever was there in order to get it. Knowing that he was doing that for me gave me the confidence I needed to be able to perform. We were a good double act.

So the first New Zealand and Australia trip was a great success – even down to my relationship with the Australian press, a very tough, independent body indeed. They had enough weight, remember, effectively to ground Frank Sinatra's private jet for a while in the early seventies because they thought he'd insulted them, so clearly you got on the wrong side of them at your peril. They were, in fact, unfailingly gentle and courteous with me, and at the end of our tour they awarded me a certificate as the Most Co-operative Artist of the Year.

We came back via Honolulu, where we had a short holiday. That's the only way round I could have done it; I could never have a holiday *before* doing the work and could never try to take a break in the middle of a tour. Go there, get the work done and then relax, that was the only way for me. It would have been as impossible for me to enjoy a holiday immediately before a major new project as it would have been for me to eat a big meal before a concert.

The return via the Pacific meant that we had literally flown round the world, and I'm glad Virginia was able to share the experience. Afterwards, while she went off to secretarial college, as planned, I carried on, perhaps not quite so hectically as before, now that The Beatles were in power, but with enough to keep me occupied – occasional TV guest spots, recordings (in rapid succession I moved around inside the EMI organization, from MGM to Columbia to HMV), Sunday concerts and plenty of appearances in Scandinavia and Holland.

Virginia, by then seventeen, came with us on our second journey to Australia and New Zealand, which followed very much the pattern set by the first, but the third time, we went without her.

It was a very different engagement in that instead of rushing from place to place often several thousand miles apart, I did four consecutive weeks at an enormous ex-service club just outside Sydney, called the St George's League, where they packed about three thousand people in every night. I still didn't run the risks of sunbathing and swimming, but just being in the one place, with a day off a week, made the whole thing very much more relaxed and casual.

In the mid-sixties I went to South Africa for the first time, a trip which was part professional, part personal, since Harry had a sister in Johannesburg and visiting her was half the idea of going. Tours in South Africa for me have been very much associated with ex-service people, in particular an organization known as the MOTHS – the Memorable Order of Tin Hats – and my audiences were made up very largely of people with some wartime connections. Out there in those days of apartheid you still had to do separate concerts for white and coloured audiences. Once again, the remembered comradeship of the years of common danger was what drew the people and me together and flavoured the whole of my relationship with South African audiences. At Port Elizabeth there's a holiday rest home for ex-servicemen where one of the bungalows is named after me. 'If you and Harry should ever feel like retiring, remember there's always a home here for you,' they told us.

That first tour in South Africa was pretty hard: Durban, Kimberley, Port Elizabeth, East London, Johannesburg, Cape Town, Benoni, in rapid succession, but the concerts were not as numerous and the distances not so vast as in Australia, and I suffered no ill-effects. And it was in South Africa that I experienced one of the most impressive welcomes I ever received: bagpipers to greet me at Johannesburg airport. What an extraordinary greeting that was! I can still remember driving down the road with those bagpipers playing in the background.

I've made trips to Canada several times for odd things. One was while Virginia was working in America, where she went in 1967. Her original idea was to go to New York with a girl friend and for the two of them to tour America by Greyhound bus. In the event the girl friend dropped out, so Virginia decided to go straight to Los Angeles to see if she could get a job. She landed a very good one, in fact, at Warner Brothers in Burbank, as an assistant in the production department. She even saved up enough money to come home for Christmas during her eighteen months there, while we went down from Canada to see her during a trip, which somehow gave us two days off. We always were a tight-knit family, not to be held apart unnecessarily by a few thousand miles. I next went to Canada in 1974, to Vancouver and Winnipeg, where I was made an Honorary Citizen.

I've done one-night stands for charity in New Zealand and Kenya and later relaxed my rule about 'no working holidays' to the extent of a trip on a Russian ship from Auckland to Tahiti in 1973, which required me to do only two concerts. We'd never been to Tahiti, and the opportunity seemed too good to miss. As usual the trip turned into a little more than that, because having got as far as Auckland it made sense to do a couple of concerts there. I could even have embarked on something like another Australian tour, because there was plenty of persuasion along the lines of 'You might as well do concerts in Australia while you're about it.' In the end I did just one.

You can be wearing out your vocal chords, travelling thousands of miles a week and appearing before large live audiences every other night, yet still find that unless you are on television fairly frequently, in England people think you've retired. I didn't really mind when people thought that, but it was pleasant to know that television did still want me, even in the late 1960s.

CHAPTER FOURTEEN

Everybody's Talking

Both the producer Stewart Morris and I approached the thought of my new television series in 1969 with some dread. This was the year Lulu tied for first place with 'Boom Bang-a-Bang' in the Eurovision Song Contest; *Star Trek* had just aired on television for the first time; David Bowie released the single, 'Space Oddity', and the Woodstock festival took place in the US. Times were changing fast and I wasn't sure I would still be right for them. For my part I was nervous, for although I'd put in guest appearances here and there during the sixties, I had been off travelling for so long that it was seven years since I'd faced the cameras with a programme of my own. In that time the music had changed, television had changed, I had probably changed and for all I knew the audience had changed, too. Stewart's problem was less complicated: he simply didn't want to work with me.

It was a long time before I could get the whole story out of him, but apparently when Bill Cotton Jr, of BBC television, asked him to produce the next Vera Lynn series, his first reaction was: 'Not on your life.' His tastes and mine had nothing in common, he thought; I was from a different era of entertainment altogether, and his new ideas and my set ways would collide head on. It could only be a disaster. But Bill Cotton went on to make it plain that whether he fancied the idea or not, he would be doing it anyway. So Stewart then resorted to that old, old dodge of believing that if he simply did nothing about it, it would go away. Except for an encounter at a show business luncheon (an encounter which I suspect was engineered by Bill Cotton), when he found himself sitting next to me and Harry and passed the time in embarrassed silence, he studiously avoided contacting us, convinced that in the end Bill Cotton would have to bow to the inevitable and put somebody else on it. Bill Cotton didn't, of course, and it gradually dawned on Stewart that short of fleeing the country he was going to have to do it.

By this time Harry was starting to get anxious, but Bill kept reassuring him – 'Not to worry, he's going to do it.' Finally, with only a few weeks to go, we met to discuss the series, and Stewart put his last card on the table. He insisted that we should forget all about the severe blouses and skirts of the previous series and go for dresses, very feminine dresses; and he wanted me to sing a lot of the songs that had been written during the sixties. To his bafflement I eagerly agreed. Oh God, he thought, she's going to co-operate; that's going to make it even harder. Without realizing it, I'd destroyed his only hope of escape, for he could no longer go back to Bill and complain that I didn't get on with him. So he decided to make the best of a bad job – and we ended up making more than half-a-dozen series together.

The fact was, of course, that I'd been away from large-scale television for so long that I had to rely on Stewart's judgement much more than I would have done earlier. It was him who thought of using the Young Generation dance troupe, for instance, who became a hugely popular part of the show. And where I would have been certain, a few years before, of the kind of musical director any programme of mine needed, I now had to have some guidance. I couldn't have been luckier, for Alyn Ainsworth proved to be the best possible MD I could have had for television at that time. He was the one who got the Young Generation singing as well as dancing; with fantastic skill and patience he would take them through the songs line by line, getting their phrasing right, helping them to feel at ease with a lyric. They later went on to get their own television show.

As far as material was concerned, there were indeed plenty of great songs in existence, but you had to have new ones as well. Interestingly, though, whereas the position had begun to look hopeless in the early sixties, by the time the new series began in 1969 there had been an improvement and a new type of song had come in, which, while it was quite different from what I had been used to singing, at least had the virtues I was familiar with – strong melodies and lyrics that had some logic to them. Stewart Morris got me singing things I would never have done off my own bat, and in some ways it was like starting again, for the metre of the new songs was different, and the construction of the lyrics less formal: they were much more like prose poems. The types of story the new songs told were different, too, and very varied, and I had to be careful that they were right for me. I had to come up to date, but in my own way and at my own pace; I had to know how far I could 'lean out' from my old self. I had some new favourites on this show: 'Everybody's Talking At Me' and 'Windmills of My Mind'.

This new song policy of Stewart's led to the making of an LP called *Hits of the Sixties*. I loved doing it: it was refreshing, it was different. I worked on it with Barry Booth, who gave me the feel of the numbers, and I found myself at ease with songs like 'By the Time I Get to Phoenix' and 'Fool on the Hill' and 'Everybody's Talking'. In terms of sheer enjoyment it was one of the best things I ever did in my career, and I think the people who bought it sensed my enjoyment.

I now have a curious feeling about the TV shows themselves. I never really enjoyed television the way I do a concert, but I loved the rehearsal for it; I appreciated that feeling of getting organized; that wonderful period when the programme is still being created and all the various elements of it are gradually coming together. The atmosphere in rehearsal – an atmosphere of work being done – was marvellous. I liked the meetings at which Stewart and Harry and Alyn and I threw songs and titles and ideas at each other. I loved to watch choreographer Nigel Lythgoe working out the movements, fitting me into the pattern of the Young Generation, keeping it all mobile. (Much later, of course, Lythgoe went on to become 'Nasty Nigel' on *Pop Idol* and a producer on *American Idol*.)

I'm proud to say that I enjoyed a marvellous relationship with the studio crew, and we always tried to get the same people for each series. Once again, it was like family: being with the people you knew and trusted made everything so much easier. It had been just the same back in the earlier series with Albert Stevenson. After we'd been together for fifty programmes they wanted to make some kind of presentation, so in the end they awarded me the Studio Bucket – one of those gigantic bucket-shaped studio ashtrays – and had an immense group photograph taken, like the passing-out class of some academy. In actual fact, we went on to do a total of seventy-eight programmes. I still have that funny old coal bucket with the inscription, 'To Vera Lynn, from all her friends at the BBC, 2nd July 1959.' I do love a roaring fire in the winter and, as you can imagine, now that I'm in my nineties, I still make a lot of use of it.

If for me the fun of television was largely over before the actual recording of the programme, you may wonder why I did much television at all. The thing was, however much I always loved radio, there was no arguing with the fact that television became *the* medium by the 1960s; if you had any feelings about your own progress it's where you had to go if the opportunity came. If you felt that you and an audience belonged to each other, it was the only way to reach them. Apart from that, in selecting the work I took on in the 1960s and 1970s I was guided largely by a combination of instinct and mood. I could usually tell very quickly if a job was going to be congenial or not; if it looked 'clear', then I did it; if it was 'cloudy' in my vision, I wouldn't touch it. In this respect you could say that I lived in a state of semi-retirement for some time, in the sense that the work I did was not done because I had to. I selected what I wanted to do, and while my health lasted and as long as I enjoyed it, I went on like that.

My career almost came to an enforced stop in June 1970, as a matter of fact. I'd been feeling unwell for some time, though there was nothing specifically wrong with me that I could put my finger on. 'Run down' is the term we usually console ourselves with, and for a while I was content to leave it at that. But when it dragged on, getting worse rather than better, I made an appointment to see my doctor. I arranged it for a day when I was going into town anyway for a recording session; psychologically I couldn't have chosen a worse moment.

When he'd finished putting me through a lot of tests, he told me I was suffering from an affliction not uncommon among trumpet players and singers, a condition of the lung called emphysema. Its effect is to make the elasticity of the lungs unreliable, and its victims often find themselves having to struggle for breath. He warned me that I might never be able to sing again, and ordered me there and then not to sing a note for four months, not even in the bath. For somebody on their way to a recording session that was bad news. Since there seemed no way out of it at such short notice, he grudgingly allowed me to go on and do that one, but I had to come to terms with the idea that it could well be my last. I suppose if I was really going to have to stop I couldn't have chosen a better song to end on, for the number I recorded that day was 'My Way', but it didn't make it any easier.

As luck would have it, when the four months' silence was over, the doctor said that provided I strictly limited the amount of work I took on, there was no reason why I shouldn't continue. I settled into another whirl of engagements, TV specials and concerts, but as time went on, during the course of the 1970s, and as I approached my sixtieth birthday in 1977, I began to slow down as a performer and tended to do less and less, until one day I simply phased my way out. That was always my intention, to fade away discreetly, and I think I managed it pretty well. I was certainly not one for dramatic retirements, endless farewell tours and perpetual comebacks, though I always wanted to carry on as long as I could when it came to charity performances. (Although I never quite imagined that I would still be doing these in my late seventies!)

Variety artists, as a body, seem to be the most ready of all to give their services to charity, and I'm proud to belong to that side of the profession. From wartime onwards, it was one of the most important parts of my work. Where a millionaire can give money to worthy causes, performers can, and do, give their arts and skills in order to raise money. Even as far back as the Ambrose days there were always fêtes and garden parties and other fundraising activities to be supported, and it's been a guiding principle of my life to help wherever I can. This made me aware from my early career that it was essential to preserve my value to charity, and that led straight back to this business of selecting the right kind of professional, paid work. If you appeared everywhere, in every kind of show and environment, you would eventually become so commonplace that people wouldn't go out of their way to see you, even if it was for a good cause. So the prestige of the commercial work you did actually reflected on your status as an aid to charity. When you did a job for charity, whether a big nationally known one or something small and local, you had to be able to do it as much good as possible.

Through my wartime connections with the armed forces, it's been a natural thing for me to support ex-service charities of all kinds. In the course of doing these benefit shows over the years I've been privileged to meet great men of the calibre of Earl Mountbatten, Lord Montgomery, General Sir William Slim and Douglas Bader. I think I also learned something about human nature from them. The predominant atmosphere at a gathering like that of the Burma Star Association at the Royal Albert Hall is one of comradeship. The son of one of those men was once talking to me, describing how he'd been present with his father at some such function. 'When you began to speak,' he told me, 'I saw a look come into my dad's eyes that I envied; I could tell that he'd experienced something valuable that I'd missed.' It seems awful that there has to be a threat before people will draw together, but as I see it the world will go on tearing itself to pieces until some danger appears from right outside it. I'm certain, though, that man needs a common enemy to unite against.

Dissension between people is particularly hard to understand for a person with such a strong sense of family as myself. Perhaps I've been lucky to be able to combine a life in entertainment with a life as a member of a family. I tried to regulate my work according to the various stages of Virginia's growing up, but there was something stronger than that at work too. Aware of the intensity and importance of my own childhood memories, I wanted to see that Virginia had the chance to develop some of her own. I sought to give her her own Weybourne by taking her into the Farnham countryside, by staying at the Bush Hotel in Farnham and making a great treat of it, and it worked. To this day the aroma of a cigar reminds her of being in the big panelled coffee room of the Bush after dinner, where Harry would puff quietly away and Virginia, then about six, would enjoy staying up late, and that curious sense of security small children get from the company of grown-ups. It's the foundation of an awareness of a family circle, and as Virginia grew older, she continued to enjoy being with her family at an age when it's now fashionable for parents and children to have grown apart. The idea was never forced on her; in fact Virginia has so much of her father in her that I can't see anyone forcing very much on her. But without in any sense sheltering in it, she did seem to prefer the family circle to anything outside it for a long time. She decided, of her own accord, not to make a break until she was twenty-one. Then she felt ready, and went to America. We never forced her towards the business, and she certainly realized at an early age that she hadn't the temperament to be an entertainer herself. Nonetheless she liked being close to the profession, and has mainly worked on the edges of it. That still didn't stop her, though, from going to Italy as an au pair in order to learn Italian when she felt the time had come to do that.

While she was young and living at home, I was far less strict with her than my mother had been with me. She was, in some strange way, strict with herself. I didn't tell her what time she had to be in. It worked the other way round – she would tell me what time she was coming home, and stick to it. The American poet Robert Frost wrote a wonderful line somewhere to the effect that 'friends are people you don't have to deserve'. I feel rather like that about family relationships. The ties between us are not obligations but pleasures. Obligations are subtle things, and while they do exist within families, they should exert their influence everywhere in life. In my own work there were the obligations of the performer to the public. They meant a good deal more than turning up, doing as well as you could and giving value for money. A star is nothing more than someone who has been singled out by the public for special attention. That in itself is a privilege, and there are many other privileges, but with them come obligations. If you accept public acclaim and all that goes with it, you must be ready to accept some degree of public scrutiny as well.

Any form of recognition is a thrill, but there's an especial thrill about receiving an honour in one of the annual Honours Lists. After all, it's an acknowledgement from the highest authority in the land, and a genuine honour, not just a formality. I usually get more nervous than excited on any special occasion, but when I went up to Buckingham Palace for my OBE in 1968, for once my excitement overruled my nerves; I was just thrilled and excited, like a child.

It was on that occasion that I was the victim of a very pleasant surprise which nearly didn't come off. After the ceremony I was inveigled up to the Martini Terrace – that suite of beautiful rooms of Martini & Rossi's at the top of New Zealand House – on the pretext of being asked to judge some competition or other. When I got there I was led into a room where the Stars Foundation for Cerebral Palsy, to which I've belonged since it started in 1955 – I was one of the founder members – had thrown a surprise party for me. There were about a hundred and fifty people there, mostly from the profession, and, to cap it all, in the middle of it in walked the Duke of Edinburgh. Apparently he'd been at Sandringham and got to hear that the party was being planned through Lady Westmoreland, and finding that originally he hadn't been invited, he invited himself. By so doing he accidentally nearly ruined the surprise, for at the Palace briefing which had preceded the investiture earlier in the day, Prince Philip's equerry started to say to me, 'See you later on at the party', but just checked himself before the cat was completely out of the bag.

I find it odd to have been writing about the Queen and the Duke of Edinburgh and the Queen Mother in this familiar way, because by nature I am in awe of authority, a great respecter of office and the last person to take liberties. Yet the members of our royal family have this knack of making you sufficiently at ease to feel you know them. It's that unfailing ability to say the right thing that does it. Improbable though it seems, Harry and I did occasionally meet the Duke of Edinburgh at show-business and ex-service functions, and his conversation on those occasions was always an object lesson in how to strike the right level. He once surprised and delighted us, years ago, when the subject of families had cropped up, by saying something to the effect that: 'We're concerned about Anne at the moment, trying to get her to make up her mind what she wants to do.' When that happens, suddenly you're not talking to your Queen's consort but to another parent.

The Queen Mother created a similar impression. I found myself once at a gathering at St James's Palace which appeared to consist entirely of Anglican clergymen; there were three rooms of what looked like solid bishops. I couldn't think why I'd been invited, for there were no other people there from entertainment, nor was there anybody about that I recognized at all, and I began to suspect that somebody had mixed up the mailing lists. Then the room cleared a little and the Queen Mother was led from one outstretched, official hand to another. The royal progress was going in an orderly fashion round the assembly when Her Majesty caught sight of me across the room. To the mild consternation of a dignitary or two, she came straight across to me with her hand out, saying: 'I didn't expect to see you here.' Frankly, neither did I, but I was suddenly made to feel a lot less out of place.

Most of my life, though, I've been lucky enough to be in the right place at the right time. I was booked into the right function on the right night to sing for Howard Baker; I was in the right publisher's office to hear that Joe Loss wanted a singer; I was in the right place to get to know that Charlie Kunz did also. I happened to be singing the right songs in the right kind of voice to fit the mood of the British service-man during the war. Luck very often seems to map our lives out for us, and time and again I've been fortunate. I also married the right man, who happened to have joined the right band at the right time. New Year 1975 saw what I thought was the crowning glory of my life – the DBE. The thrill of that was even bigger than my amazement that a little girl from East Ham could actually become a dame. I didn't imagine then that I'd still have another thirty years left to go ...

CHAPTER FIFTEEN

Never Quite Retired

As the years passed and increasingly a lot of my work was focused on charity, I ended up getting one hat trick I'm very proud of: three Royal Variety shows across three decades – in 1960, 1975 and 1986. And I'm able to say that I have performed with some of the favourites of the last century: Bing Crosby, Morecambe and Wise, Cliff Richard. I became Chairwoman of the Breast Cancer Research Trust in 1976 and have been ever since. Having been involved with cerebral palsy charities since the 1950s, I continued to raise money for them throughout the 1970s and 1980s and was eventually to found my own charity, the Dame Vera Lynn Trust for Children with Cerebral Palsy, in 2001. It has been a real pleasure for me in later life to be involved with the Dame Vera Lynn School for Parents, in West Sussex, which is financed entirely through voluntary contributions. The school is a unique place where young children with cerebral palsy, and other disabilities, learn daily living skills alongside their parents through conductive education. I'm a regular visitor and thrilled to see the school doing so well.

My daughter Virginia has helped me with a lot of these activities, especially in recent years. But often as early as the

1970s she would attend events on my behalf and she still remembers a symposium in the early days of the Breast Cancer Research Trust where she brought up the idea – then very new – of tackling the psychological problems of dealing with this disease.

People sometimes ask me why I didn't have any more children: Virginia was my only child. We are very close – she is 'Verge' to me. And although she is in her sixties now (which I can't believe!) she still calls me Mamma. When Harry died in 1998 we became even closer. We always got on but now we are great friends. We tell each other off now too. Virginia says that age has a lot to do with it. The older you get as a daughter, the more you are your own person. We're more like equals than ever now. Although I live in my own house, Virginia is next door and I go to her house two or three times a week for supper.

The fact is, if I was going to have any more children it would have been in the post-war years, and it just turned out that I was very busy then. So it just didn't happen for me – if I'd had more children I would not have been able to continue working. That's just how it was. Because Harry had been invalided out of the Squadronnaires, effectively I was the breadwinner.

I suppose you could say that Virginia has also been a career woman. She now works as a complementary health therapist, but throughout the 1970s and 1980s she had many exciting and glamorous jobs in the worlds of fashion and media (she was a television researcher for many years, including a stint on Michael Parkinson's television show). Partly because of her work, she didn't get married until she was forty.

Her husband, Tom, who's now in his late sixties, was in the RAF and had been married before, so Virginia inherited a grown-up step-daughter, Tesni. Thanks to Tesni, Virginia has three grandchildren, Tobi, Sam and Lucy, whom I regard as my great-grandchildren. They call me Nanny DV. Virginia had wanted to have children of her own, but unfortunately she kept having miscarriages. She had eight in the end. It was awful. It still makes us all very sad to think about it. As Virginia says, everybody wants their own child with somebody that they love, but what can you do? You just have to get on with it.

I now feel very lucky to have Virginia and Tom living so close to me. They married in October 1986 and moved in next door in 1995, a few years before Harry died. He had angina and died when there were complications after an operation. He had a stroke and never recovered. We had been married for fifty-seven years when he died. I grieved for him terribly – he was the love of my life. But it gave me some comfort at least that we had such a long and happy life together. And I am thrilled that Virginia has a husband she feels the same way about.

I don't want to take credit for Virginia meeting her husband, but it's true that they more or less met through me. Virginia first met Tom when he landed in our back field in a Chinook helicopter that was due to take me to a charity fête in 1982. Tom was one of the RAF officers on board. We gave them tea at home afterwards. They met again years later when Tom asked Virginia, at the BBC, to help his daughter out because she was thinking about working for that company.

Although we are small in number, family life is hugely important to me. But I have been lucky enough to have all sorts of engagements to keep me busy since my professional life slowed down. Looking back, the high point of my career came in 1975. And it was quite an exclamation mark to what was then forty years in show business. Receiving the letter from Buckingham Palace about the DBE was definitely one of the highlights of that time and probably of my whole life. They write to you to ask if you will accept the honour and you're supposed to write back. Of course, I was thrilled – because it is quite a thrill to know that you have been recognized for everything that you've been doing.

When I received the award I went to a small dinner party in London and the Queen Mother asked me how my mother was, as she often did. On that occasion she stretched out her hand and gave me a marron glacé and said, 'Take this for your mother.' My mother was thrilled to have been remembered in this way. It was not long after this that my mother died, well into her eighties by this point. In the end she broke her hip and was taken into hospital, where she developed pneumonia. I had her brought down from Barking in an ambulance to stay in a hospital near us, which is where she died. I was glad that she had seen me succeed in my career – the path she had set me off on all those years ago. Both my parents supported me throughout my entire career, although after the war they didn't come to my concerts as much, as I was travelling a lot and they were getting too old to come. But they were very proud of me – my dad especially. I know what he thought of it all: 'My little girl makes good.' My brother Roger has also always been a great support to me. After his time in the RAF when he serviced the Spitfires during the Battle of Britain (he was up for three days and three nights without going to bed), he ran a grocery shop and later went into the music publishing business. We are still good friends and he lives a twenty-minute drive away.

Because we were a royalist family, my mother was particularly delighted to know that my performances were appreciated by royalty too – as was I, of course. I have never felt comfortable saying that I knew the Queen Mother well – you feel too much respect to say something like that. But I was very privileged to enjoy her company on many occasions. The Queen Mother was especially relaxed and informal – she and I could just sit down and chat. You would not do that with the Queen: she has always been more official in her duties. I always loved, incidentally, the way the Queen Mother had a very recognizable way of dressing. I used to know her to turn up in quite cold weather in one of her floaty chiffon dresses – she loved chiffon. Sometimes I used to wonder, isn't it a bit chilly to wear something like that? Her clothes were always that same wonderful style – those loose duster coats were very appropriate for her. And she had such fantastic hats. In all the times we met I don't think I once saw her in a tailored outfit.

In particular I always loved performing for the royal family at the Royal Variety shows at the Palladium. All performers love going in front of the royal family. It's a form of recognition for your work, and you have the opportunity to meet them afterwards. What I discussed with the Queen Mother depended on the situation. When my daughter was young and so was

Prince Charles, we would talk about families. She would ask me about working with a young child, or about my music, because Charles loved music. She asked after my mother when she was ill. But if we were at an official function, we would talk about that. One time when we were together at the unveiling of the monument to the war at St Paul's, and we talked about the people of London and how wonderful they were.

When the Queen Mother died in March 2002 at the age of 101, I was extremely upset. I had sent her a message of sympathy at the end of the previous year when she was very ill. We had enjoyed some good times together. I took part in her 100th birthday parade the previous year. (That was quite an occasion, incidentally: I had tea at St James's Palace, rode in a tank, and Virginia and Tom got their picture on the front page of *The Times*, sitting behind Prince Charles, looking at The Wombles.) I think what was so special about the Queen Mother was that she really loved people. She loved being with people and it meant a great deal to her. She was such a friendly, warm personality and she treated everyone as an individual, not as part of the crowd. She spoke to you personally as if you were the only person there. This warmth just came radiating out of her. During the war people had a great respect for the lovely family feeling she had about her. People tend to forget now that during the Blitz she stayed in the UK when she could have gone abroad: she mingled with people on the bomb sites and that counted for a lot. I think that is what endeared her to everybody – giving them courage and making them feel that they were at one with the royal family. It helped them to believe there was this togetherness.

It gives me so much pleasure that the Queen Mother was present for many of the highlights of my career. My last public performance in May 1995 was quite a day, both happy and sad for me: the last time I was ever to sing officially in public – at the age of seventy-eight. It was an auspicious occasion: the golden jubilee of VE Day at Hyde Park and Buckingham Palace. I have no regrets about that being my last perform- ance. I felt that I had sung for long enough. That was a good time to finish. I wanted to leave with good memories and not wait till I couldn't sing any more. I never sing now – not even at home. Your voice does not stand up to doing a solo after all those years. That was such a great day, though. The Mall was choc-a-bloc on both sides.

Funny to think that there were more high points to come, though. Just as I thought I had properly retired, I would find myself attending more anniversaries. One of the highlights of recent years was in May 2005 when thousands gathered in Trafalgar Square for a concert to celebrate the sixtieth anniversary of VE Day. Katherine Jenkins was there – who I think is a wonderful young singer – and she performed several wartime songs, including 'We'll Meet Again'. Although, as I said, I hate to sing in public now – the voice is just not there any more – I joined in with a few bars of the chorus. I gave a speech in honour of the veterans, reminding the younger generation never to forget the sacrifices they made for their country and our freedom.

Katherine Jenkins was there again for my ninetieth birth- day celebrations in 2007 at a lunchtime reception at the Imperial War Museum and I said to her then: 'Once you get in the troops' good books, they never forget you.' That was an amazing day: I was lucky enough to have amongst my guests June Whitfield, Bill Pertwee, Liz Smith, Frank Thornton, Baroness Boothroyd, ballerina Darcey Bussell and Baroness Thatcher, all singing Happy Birthday to me. Can you imagine? And this was supposed to be my quiet retirement. I do enjoy looking back on all the famous people I have worked with. Morecambe and Wise were particularly lovely. They were very funny and relaxed off stage. Cliff Richard is a lovely man too – very easy going and friendly.

Looking back on my engagements diary for the past ten years, there have been all sorts of landmarks I never dared hope I would reach. In October 2003 there was another meeting with the Queen for the opening of the 'Women at War' exhibition at the Imperial War Museum; in June 2006, a special birthday lunch for the Queen's eightieth birthday alongside the likes of then Prime Minister Tony Blair, Baroness Thatcher, Sir John Major, guitarist Eric Clapton and – a good friend – Sir Cliff Richard.

I didn't look forward to retirement really, because work was all I had ever known. I know I could have stopped earlier but I always felt I was doing something useful. It was obvious that people enjoyed my singing and I enjoyed meeting the veterans, and having a chat with the Burma boys. At one occasion at the Imperial War Museum there was a veteran from Burma who had kissed me on the cheek when I was on tour out there. They got him to kiss me again sixty years on. It's nice to look back and think that you had the opportunity to collect memories like that.

I always think now, though, that I left my retirement too late. Imagine giving up singing at the age of seventy-eight! When you wait that long to retire you find that there are things that you want to do and when you get to a certain age, you can't do them. I would have liked to travel a bit more as a normal person and not as a performer. I have been all over Europe, America and Australia for work but it would have been nice to travel more for myself, without having the responsibility of concerts. I suppose, though, that I had done a lot and seen a lot by the time I retired. And it was nice just to concentrate on things at home.

One of the things I enjoy most about retirement is just that: being at home. I like keeping in touch with the services and attending charity events, but I do like visiting friends and being able to go out to places and just walk around without having to be involved in cutting any ribbons. I didn't have time to do things like that all my working life. I rarely had time for doing things for my own pleasure. Time was always taken up doing something. That's why I suppose I enjoy it so much now when I do go and visit gardens and places. I know I'm free.

I used to garden myself but I'm afraid I'm not able to do it now. Pots and tubs are now my biggest venture into gardening. I used to love to garden properly – digging, getting down on your hands and knees and having a really good old weed-out. But now I just do the odd jobs I can manage. I still like being busy out in the open air and I'm not fussy about plants: I like anything that flowers. Some people are mad about roses and I agree that they're beautiful. But I like everything. Years ago I used to have a little vegetable patch, but it got to the point where I couldn't cope with it any more. I used to love growing beans and blackcurrants.

Gardening was something I always liked because I remember as a small child I made a rockery at the bottom of the garden in East Ham. Back then, in my mind I dreamt of having a house with a big garden. I used to walk to school in those days – a long way and always on foot no matter what the weather – and I would stop and admire the gardens of the houses on the way: we only had a privet hedge at the front of the house, and the back garden was paved with my tiny little rockery at the back. I have a lovely photograph of me in that garden aged about eight, wearing a white shift dress and Mary Jane shoes and with a page-boy haircut. Happy times.

There are many compensations to old age, though. It's wonderful to be able to look back and reflect on a long and fulfilled life. It's funny to think that in my day it wasn't all organized the way it is now. You were a singer – that was your life. You were offered jobs and you took them or you didn't. We just did our job, took what dates were offered. The BBC offered you programmes, you got a contract … It was much more natural than it is now. Things just happened. I never had an agent who went out selling me. I never looked for work. Requests just came in. And there wasn't the merchandising they have now.

Image was a completely different thing in those days too. You were aware that you were well known: you had your fan mail to cope with. And it meant a lot to people to have a letter from you and a photograph. During the war I sent out literally thousands of letters and pictures. You just did it all yourself. I didn't have a manager taking care of all that as they would nowadays.

Of course, I cared about the way that I looked, but I never planned to have a certain image. When I was a child I hated having my photograph taken and there are so many pictures of me scowling. But I had to get to like it once I was in the profession. Women in the profession always tried to look glamorous; it was part of the job to make sure you looked nice wherever you went, whether you were on stage or not. You were in the public eye, so you always wanted to be looking nice. I think one took more notice of one's appearance than some of the stars do today. They go about in trousers and sloppy jackets and cardigans. They're much more casual. In my day you were much more dressy. You always wore a hat and gloves. I was brought up to wear gloves. That sounds old-fashioned now, but that's how it was.

Looking back on the past ninety-plus years, I think the 1950s were the best years. It was a much slower life then; life was quieter. People didn't want as much because it just wasn't there after the war. The more there is in the world to have, the more people want it. Some things are much better now and some are not so good. Are people happier now? I don't think so. Back then people were more contented. But that's progress, isn't it? Everything moves on. In the 1950s everyone was relaxed. We were all thrilled the war was over. We still had rationing up to a point: food was rationed until 1954 and petrol was rationed on and off until 1957. But you could drive wherever you wanted in comfort in those days; there just wasn't the traffic you have now. It was as though we returned to the pre-war era.

These days I feel there is such a lot to be had and everyone – quite naturally – wants to get the most they can of whatever's going. The pace of life is so much quicker and there are more people than ever. Everything always seems so busy. Everywhere grows, towns grow, villages grow and everything gets more and more and bigger and bigger … When there is less overall, life is quieter and more peaceful. There is not so much for people to want. And it's a question of what you don't have, you don't miss.

There was a lot that was terrible about those times during and after the war, though. I have sad and happy memories. But people pulled together and they didn't want things they couldn't have, as everybody does nowadays. It was a much simpler life. There wasn't so much around that people could think to themselves, I want this and I want that. If we wanted something we had to save up for it and we couldn't buy it unless we had the money for it. I suppose there were always people who used to buy things on the 'never-never', as we called it, but unless I had the money for something, I didn't buy it. I never borrowed money. The only time I ever borrowed anything was when I bought my first house on a mortgage – and I never rested until I had paid it off. It took me two years.

Sometimes, though, I think that times and people have not changed so much. If a world war broke out, I'm sure there'd be no problem. You'd naturally get a few chaps who would cry off, but on the whole we Brits are a patriotic and sentimental lot. I'm sure the young people today would do the same as those in the forties. If we had to go to war now, I think we could cope very well. When the Brits are against the wall, that's when they start coming forward.

War of the sort we had in the 1940s sometimes feels – thankfully – a very remote idea, though. I'm not sure young people these days can imagine what it was like. I feel sad sometimes that memories of the old days have already been lost. Over the last few years they have been teaching more in schools about the Second World War, but it took so long for the schools to get around to it that a lot of living history was lost. It was left too long, and memories fade. Now that generation is dying out and we are losing contact with the past. If they had started properly in schools even ten or fifteen years ago, then schoolchildren would have heard some wonderful stories.

For me personally I see now that the highlight of my life was having the opportunity to go to Burma to entertain the boys myself. It was an experience I would have hated to miss. After years of singing to them on the radio, I so much wanted to sing to them in person, to witness the conditions they were living in, to live the same way as them, to experience the same food, accommodation and atmosphere … It happened because I volunteered – you were never asked to do these things – and I suppose I did that because I almost felt a bit guilty, getting all these letters from the boys at war. I just had this feeling that I had to see them in person. I appreciated so much what they were doing, fighting for their country. I felt I wanted to be alongside them for a while.

I had never imagined that I would have an experience like that in my life. It seems funny to me now that the first thought

I had when I heard over the radio, sitting in the garden in East Ham with my mum and dad, that war had been declared was, Bang goes my career. There won't be any entertainment. Everything will close down and stop. I'll be off to the munitions factory. Which ended up, of course, being the opposite to what happened.

I feel so lucky that I genuinely don't have any regrets in my life. There is nothing to regret in my personal life. I married a lovely man and had a lovely daughter. We were very happy, my husband and I, before he died. I have tried to be useful in my own way. And I feel I've had the opportunity to make the most of my life.

I think I feel satisfied because I never had any mad ambitions, even in my younger days. I only wanted to be the best singer in the biggest band – and I achieved that with Ambrose. Apart from that, I never had a burning desire to do much. As long as I was occupied doing something and people were enjoying my singing, I was happy. And I was thankful that I had the opportunities. I just happened to be the singer whose voice suited the time and fitted in with the situation. A lot of people don't have that chance. They have the talent and the intelligence, but they just don't come at the right time. There's a time for everything and if you're lucky enough that your time comes along and you can enjoy it ... well, you're very lucky indeed. It's so different now from when I was young. All I can say is, take advantage of the opportunities. Make up your mind what you want to do, and go and get it. Make sure it is not at the expense of anyone else, though: it'll always come back on you. If you're going up the ladder, be nice to the people that you pass on the way: you may meet them on your way back down. That's what I've always said.

In another way I feel very fortunate in that I've never had to stop doing what I love. I just keep on going. Even now that I'm in my early nineties there is barely a week goes by that I'm not off to open a fête or cut a ribbon somewhere. It's flattering to get so many requests and I really enjoy it. I also find it unbelievable that I still get fan mail and thank-you letters from all over the world. Some of them are addressed to 'Vera Lynn, England' and they still manage to find their way here. Only the other day I received a letter wishing me 'sunny greetings from Uzbekistan', asking me to contribute to their Peace Autograph Project and write a message of peace. I wrote back: 'I sincerely hope that the mistakes that we made in the past will always be recalled and that we will work for a brighter and more peaceful future.'

What is left of my own memories now that I'm in my tenth decade? Fortunately an awful lot. I have so many of them. I keep one of my favourite photographs of the Queen Mother in my sitting room, where I look at it often. The picture captures us sharing a joke. We had quite a few giggles together over the years. Behind us, a guardsman is looking on fondly, as if to say, 'Take a look at these two.' Although I wouldn't for a minute put myself in the same category as the royal family or the Queen Mother, we certainly shared something. We survived the same era and we knew what it meant to be a symbol of that era. I keep that picture with my other favourite photographs lined up on my grand piano in my sitting room, overlooking the garden. I have been lucky enough to have been invited to all sorts of wonderful events and have portraits of some extraordinary moments. There's a lovely picture of me at the Queen's Golden Jubilee at the Royal Academy of Art in 2002, standing in royal blue with Baroness Thatcher (in shocking pink and rather a beautiful hat) and Dame Shirley Bassey. Pictures like these are on top of the piano I bought just after the war. It's not the piano I learnt my songs on as a child – we had an ordinary little upright which my mother used to play – but it holds many happy memories: I had it in the flat in London when Virginia was just one year old.

But my memory is in song as much as in pictures. People often ask me if I ever got fed up singing the same songs over and over again. I must have sung them tens of thousands of times. There were many good songs, both during the war and afterwards, when I went on tour to Australia, Canada, Norway and elsewhere. 'Yours' or 'We'll Meet Again' – I was always asked to sing those. And 'The White Cliffs of Dover': I could never that leave out – it meant so much to everyone. The white cliffs of Dover were the last thing the boys saw as they were leaving. The song meant home to them. I never minded singing those songs for one moment.

At other times people have wondered what my appeal was and why it has endured over the years. I don't really have an answer to that. At the age of ninety-two there is something uncomfortable – if flattering – about people seeing you as a 'national treasure'. Where I live locally they call me the Queen Mother of Sussex. I feel awkward about it and I tend to think it is a bit of a laugh. But it's very kind of people to think of me in that way and I'm also proud of that role – and proud that seventy years on since the outbreak of war the sacrifices of thousands are not forgotten. If people can remember that through the songs associated with me, I am glad of it.

I am very humbled by the regard in which I'm held and by how many people remember my music. I heard that there was a poll in the year 2000 in which I was voted the person 'who most represents the spirit of the last century'. No names were suggested to participants: my name just came up – to a fifth of the people who voted. Why is that? I can't say myself for sure. Maybe it's hard to understand now, because I came from a time that was so much more innocent. I think people looked at me as one of them – an ordinary girl from an ordinary family with a voice that you could recognize. It's that simple.

Index

307

INDEX

INDEX

ALSO AVAILABLE ON DVD!

THE VERA LYNN COLLECTION 3 DISC BOX SET
INCLUDING:

WE'LL MEET AGAIN
ONE EXCITING NIGHT
RHYTHM SERENADE